Destiny Held Hostage

**Freedom is God's Plan,
but It's Your Choice**

BY
Vikki Burke

Unless otherwise indicated, all Scripture quotations are taken from the *New Living Translation* of the Bible, copyright © 1996, 2004, 2007 by Tyndale House Foundation, Carol Stream, Illinois 60188.

New American Standard Bible © The Lockman Foundation 1960, 1962, 1963, 1968, 1972, 1973, 1975, 1977, La Habra, California.

The Amplified Bible © The Lockman Foundation, La Habra, California, 1954, 1958.

The New Testament in Modern English (Phillips). Rev. Ed. © 1958, 1959, 1960, 1972 by J.B. Phillips. Published by Macmillan Publishing Co., New York, New York.

The Living Bible © 1971 by Tyndale House Publishers, Inc., Wheaton, Illinois.

New International Version © 1973, 1978, 1984 by International Bible Society.

The Heart of Paul © 1976 by Ben Campbell Johnson. Published by A Great Love, Inc., Toccoa, Georgia.

Destiny Held Hostage
ISBN 978-1-890026-21-9
© 2014 by Vikki Burke
P.O. Box 150043
Arlington, TX 76015

Published by Vikki Burke
P.O. Box 150043
Arlington, TX 76015

Text Design: Lisa Simpson

All rights reserved. None of this book may be reproduced or transmitted in any form or by any means, electronic or mechanical, including photocopying, recording or by any information storage and retrieval system, without the written permission of the publisher. Printed in the United States of America.

Dedicated to my loving sister
Bonnie Chavez Morentin
who is now enjoying the ultimate freedom.

CONTENTS

Chapter 1 Your Destiny, Your Choice 7

Chapter 2 The Man Who Would Be King 27

Chapter 3 The Wise Woman and the Fool 47

Chapter 4 Never! 69

Chapter 5 The Untouchables 89

Chapter 6 It's Nothing Personal 105

Chapter 7 Don't Let the Devil Defuse Your Dream ... 123

Chapter 8 When Life Disappoints You 145

Chapter 9 It's Time to Play Some Serious Offense 167

Chapter 10 The Devil's Greatest Fear 193

Chapter 11 Unstoppable Power...or Easy Prey? 209

Chapter 12 The Place Where Destinies Go to Die 225

Chapter 13 Guard Your Heart 247

Chapter 14 Be Bold and Keep Building! 267

Chapter 15 Will You Be a Survivor...or a Champion? ... 289

1

YOUR DESTINY, YOUR CHOICE

"Haven't you realized yet that bread isn't the problem? The problem is yeast, Pharisee-Sadducee yeast."
Matthew 16:11, The Message

At 4:45 on a Friday afternoon, one sentence lit the fuse on a bomb that almost destroyed my future. On the day of my big promotion, it was the last thing I expected to hear.

My supervisor had asked to see me but I assumed she just wanted to say goodbye. Maybe even congratulate me. This was, after all, her last day and I'd been training to take over her position for months. So for both of us this was a time to celebrate. She was heading home to have her baby and I was taking her place as supervisor over the department where I worked.

All smiles, I checked off the last item on my weekly To Do list and gathered up a few files I might need for the meeting. Grabbing my purse from the desk drawer, I glanced around at the employees I'd trained, their fingers clicking on computer keys. The leadership transition would be easy. Everybody in the department knew I'd been named the new supervisor. I'd already been doing the job while at the same time keeping up with my former responsibilities. So on Monday morning when I officially stepped into the position, nothing would really change.

Including my salary.

Oh well…so what if I wasn't getting a raise? I'd achieved something and been recognized for it. Or so I thought. Then I stepped into the meeting.

I knew in an instant something was wrong. The air quivered with tension. Greeting me with a pained expression, my supervisor motioned for me to take a seat next to another employee who, it seemed, had been invited to join us.

I thought, *What is she doing here?*

For an awkward moment the three of us looked at each other in silence. Then my supervisor began to measure out her explanation, dispensing phrases like small doses of bitter medicine. "Vikki…I wanted to be the one to tell you this…It wasn't my decision….Still, I felt I owed it to you under the circumstances…It seems a last minute change has been made…"

Nodding toward the other employee, she dropped the bomb.

"She is being given the position of supervisor."

Slack-jawed, I caught my breath as if I'd just been slapped. Scrambling to make sense of the information, I searched for some reason. I couldn't think of any. Certainly this couldn't be about competency or qualifications. It couldn't be a matter of training or experience.

Then it dawned on me. *Office politics.* That's all it could be. Suddenly I knew without asking: This woman was getting the position I'd worked so hard to earn. *Don't play games with me*, I thought. *Don't pretend this woman has earned my promotion. Tell me the truth.*

But no truth was forthcoming. Instead I received one final nauseating instruction. "Starting Monday you will be training her to do your job."

Humiliated, hurt, and betrayed, I stared in stunned disbelief at my supervisor. "Fine," I said. And turning my back, I walked out of her office. And out of the building. With no intention of returning.

Ever.

As I drove home in fury I cast from my mind the fact that the Lord had clearly led me to come to work for this company. I didn't care anymore. Leaving these "traitors" without anyone to train their new political appointee was the only revenge available to me. *They can do what they want with this job,* I fumed. *I'm done.*

Dennis was out of town so I spent all of Friday night alone sobbing in pain and outrage. All day Saturday, too. On Sunday I stared at my swollen, salt-encrusted face in the mirror, decided I couldn't go to church, and cried some more. Wallowing in a bathtub of tears wasn't the norm for me. I'd been tough all my life. Had to be just to survive. But this razor cut of betrayal had caught me off guard. It hadn't been inflicted by the usual suspects—world-hardened unbelievers. It had been delivered by Christians, co-workers, people I'd trusted.

So the faucet of tears flowed and flowed.

Finally, sometime on Sunday night it dried up. That's when God, having given me some time to process the idea, spoke to me. *It's your destiny, Vikki,* He said. *You get to make the choice.*

That was not what I wanted to hear. Bristling at the thought of going back to work as if nothing had happened, I wished for once that God would keep quiet. But try as I might to shake His words, I couldn't. They clung to me like a mist, cooling the emotional fever that for the past 48 hours had clouded my thinking. *Your destiny...You get to make the choice....*

Taking a last fierce swipe at my runny nose, I announced my decision out loud to an empty house. "No one will ever steal my destiny!"

On Monday morning I went to the office and started training the woman who was taking my position. I won't kid you, it was horrible. What's worse, once she was trained I continued doing the work while she walked away with the supervisor's title. But it didn't matter. I'd made up my mind: *Nothing was worth giving somebody else control over my destiny.* So, by the grace of God, I made the right choice and stayed in the center of God's will.

Looking back now some 30 years later, it's clear to me what would have happened if I'd done otherwise. Most likely, I would have become disappointed, maybe even bitter. I might have given up ministry altogether. If disappointment had continued to rule in my heart, Dennis and I may have gotten a divorce. I was so young in the Lord, I might have even walked away from God completely.

Granted, to some degree that's conjecture. I can't say with absolute certainty how my life would have unfolded. But I do know this beyond any shadow of a doubt: If I had acted on my first impulse, I would have missed out on a major portion of God's plan for my life. Part of my destiny would have been destroyed.

Just because somebody else got my job.

IT CAN HAPPEN TO ANYBODY

My story isn't unique, of course. Christians everywhere have their own version because at one time or another most everybody is blindsided by betrayal. They're running their spiritual race, giving their all for Jesus, when some insult or injustice knocks them off course. Best case scenario, they stagger around nursing their wounds for a while (like I did) and then manage to go on. Worst case, they lose their way altogether, fail to get back on track again, and wind up falling permanently short of their God-ordained destiny.

We'd all like to believe the latter could never happen to us. But this is the truth: It can happen to anybody. In fact, the devil is planning on it. Even now he's plotting his ambushes. He's setting up strategies designed to derail each and every one of us. Jesus warned us about it in the Bible. He said in Luke 17:1:

> At one time or another most everybody is blindsided by betrayal.

- "It is inevitable that stumbling blocks should come" (NASB).
- "Temptations (snares, traps set to entice to sin) are sure to come" (AMP).
- "Hard trials…are bound to come" (The Message).
- "It is impossible but that offences will come" (KJV).

If we're smart, we'll get ready to handle those things. We'll arm ourselves in advance with the wisdom of God so we won't be caught off guard when something or somebody slaps us in the face. We'll strap on our scriptural track shoes now so that down the road, when we're sprinting along and the devil tries to trip us, we won't go sprawling. We'll be sure-footed enough to stay upright and keep on running.

"Well, I think I'm pretty well-prepared," you might say. "I know the Bible says we're not supposed to get offended. So whenever somebody hurts my feelings I just tell myself to get over it."

I'll be honest with you, that won't always cut it. When you're reeling from the pain of mistreatment it's not enough just to smack yourself, like a teacher wielding a ruler, with the command, "Thou shalt not be offended." Sometimes you need something more. And, I'm glad to say, the Scriptures provide it. They're full of stories, examples, and instructions that can help you recover when your heart has been wounded. They provide wisdom that can help protect you so that you don't have to be blindsided by such wounds again...and again...and again.

You see, God knows, even if we don't, this is serious business. An offense can cause genuine harm. We tend to forget that because the word offense is tossed around so casually these days. We say someone is offended when we mean they're just over-sensitive and snippy: Like the church member who's upset with the pastor for neglecting to shake his hand. Or the wife who sulks because her husband rushed off to work without kissing her goodbye.

A missed handshake or peck on the cheek can be shrugged off with ease as no big deal. But a real offense can't.

Check out the definition of the word and you'll see why. According to the dictionary, *to offend* means *to violate, transgress against, attack, or assault; to hurt, anger, shock, and cause to stumble.* You might as well tell a cancer patient to "just get over it" as to say to someone who has experienced such things to simply ignore them and go on. No can do, my friend.

Actually, the Greek word used in the New Testament for offense is: *skandalon*. It refers to a snare, something that trips up or lures into sin. In a literal, physical sense, it can refer to a trap-stick.

What, exactly, is a trap-stick? According to Thayer's Greek Lexicon, it's *the movable stick or trigger of a trap, an impediment placed in the way and causing one to stumble or fall.* I envision it as a rod positioned to prop up a cage so that when an animal touches it, the cage drops and becomes a prison.

> Satan exploiting our pain, anger, shock, and disappointment, he trips us into saying or doing something we shouldn't. That's when the cage falls and he says: *Gotcha!*

That's a perfect picture of the snares Satan sets up for us as believers. He baits us with hurts, betrayals, and injustices. Then he endeavors to trap us with our own reactions. Exploiting our pain, anger, shock, and disappointment, he trips us into saying or doing something we shouldn't. That's when the cage falls and he says:

Gotcha!

Thank God, when we do stumble into such snares there is a way of escape. We'll talk about that in the coming chapters. But it's not primarily what this book is about. This book is about avoiding the trap altogether. It's about identifying the danger before you trip the trigger so that you can avoid the trap and live free all the time.

Freedom is, after all, God's perfect will for us. The Bible makes it clear: "If the Son makes you free, you shall be free indeed."[1] "It is for freedom that Christ has set us free."[2] But as most of us have already discovered, such liberty isn't automatic. We don't enjoy it 24/7 just because we're born again. We have to take hold of it by faith and guard it with diligence.

We have to learn, as Jesus said, to "beware of the yeast."

IT'S NOT ABOUT THE BREAD

If you have no idea what it means to beware of yeast, you're in good company. Neither did the early disciples when Jesus said it to them. And to be honest, I wondered about it myself for a long time. *Yeast?* I thought. *What yeast?*

Searching for the answer, I read and re-read theses verses in Matthew 16:

> On the way to the other side of the lake, the disciples discovered they had forgotten to bring along bread. In the meantime, Jesus said

---
[1] John 8:36, NKJV
[2] Galatians 5:1, NIV

to them, "[Beware of and] keep a sharp eye out for Pharisee-Sadducee yeast." Thinking he was scolding them for forgetting bread, they discussed in whispers what to do. Jesus knew what they were doing and said, "Why all these worried whispers about forgetting the bread? Runt believers! Haven't you caught on yet? Don't you remember the five loaves of bread and the five thousand people [I fed with them], and how many baskets of fragments you picked up? Or the seven loaves that fed four thousand, and how many baskets of leftovers you collected? Haven't you realized yet that bread isn't the problem? The problem is yeast, Pharisee-Sadducee yeast." (vv. 7-11, The Message).

One day several years ago, as I was reading those verses for the umpteenth time, I couldn't stand to leave the question unanswered anymore: What on earth did Jesus mean?

Having cooked with yeast, I assumed I knew all there is to know about it. But since I was still unable to come up with any spiritual connotation, I decided to look up the word in the dictionary. As I read the definition, one particular fact caught my attention: Yeast is something that agitates. It's a substance that creates excitement, commotion, unrest, or boiling up. One dictionary used the phrase, *to put emotions to ferment*.

Suddenly, I understood why Jesus used the word yeast in reference to the Pharisees and Sadducees! They were always trying to agitate Him. They were continually doing and saying things that were demonically designed to provoke Him and make Him mad.

The day He warned about their "yeast," they'd been harassing Him again. They'd come to test His claims "by asking him to show them a miraculous sign from heaven."[3] Clothing themselves in religious correctness, they'd insulted Jesus and all but accused Him of fraud.

Can you imagine such a thing? Accusing Jesus of fraud? Demanding Him to perform on command and prove He's not a liar? Talk about offensive!

To make matters worse, the Pharisees' demands weren't even sincere. They already knew about the miracles Jesus had worked. They'd heard how He healed the sick, lame, maimed, and blind. How He'd fed thousands of people with a few loaves of bread and a couple of fish. They probably even witnessed some of those miracles first hand. So they knew the reports were true.

> The Pharisees and Sadducees wanted to agitate Jesus and push Him into blowing His cool so He would say something they could use against Him.

But the Pharisees and Sadducees weren't interested in the truth. What they wanted was to agitate Jesus and get a rise out of Him. They wanted to push Him into blowing His cool so He would say something they could use against Him. They meant to trick Him into

---
[3] Matthew 16:1

hanging Himself with His own words. (In Greek, the word *accuse* can literally refer to putting a noose around the neck.)

But Jesus didn't fall for it. He knew what their yeast was intended to do. So He refused to boil over with irritation and fall into their trap. Instead He simply replied:

> "You know the saying, 'Red sky at night means fair weather tomorrow, red sky in the morning means foul weather all day.' You are good at reading the weather signs in the sky, but you can't read the obvious signs of the times! Only an evil, faithless generation would ask for a miraculous sign, but the only sign I will give them is the sign of the prophet Jonah." Then Jesus left them and went away. (vv. 2-4)

In other words, Jesus stayed calm in the face of the Pharisees' insults. He told them there was no point in showing them anything because they were too steeped in spiritual darkness to see. Then, saying a simple no to their demand for a sign, He just walked away.

Wouldn't you like to respond with that kind of composure when you're under pressure?

Sure you would.

Me too. And we could do it if we'd learn to beware of the yeast.

But then...that's the problem.

Most of us don't recognize yeast when we encounter it. We react to situations that agitate us before we realize what's happening. We get angry at people who mistreat us without taking into account that the devil is using them as bait.

As a result, we find ourselves entrapped by offense again and again.

By definition, *entrapment* takes place when a person is induced or persuaded to commit an act he had no previous intention of committing. It's what sometimes happens to us, for example, on Sundays after church. We walk out after the service so innocent. We love God. We're feeling good, singing and praising and enjoying the presence of the Lord. Our hearts are uplifted and we have no intention of acting ugly toward anybody.

Then on the way home, a guy in a rusted out pick-up cuts in front of us on the freeway. He's going 45 instead of 65, suffocating us with exhaust fumes, and we can't get around him. We slam on the horn and the truck driver responds with a one-finger salute. Our spouse freaks and launches into a lecture about the dangers of road rage while the kids start wailing in the back seat. Suddenly we're saying things we couldn't have imagined 20 minutes ago. Things we would never say in church.

Later, when we're trying to patch things up with our spouse and comfort the kids, we think, *How did this happen? How did I let one slow truck ruin my entire Sunday?*

By adding yeast, that's how! It puffed up the situation and made it look bigger than it really was. If we hadn't added the yeast, if we hadn't yielded to the agitation, the incident would have stayed small, flat, and insignificant. It wouldn't have affected us at all.

WILL YOU BE GEORGE OR BENEDICT?

If yeast only bothered us during minor traffic troubles it might not be worth writing a book about. But as I've already said, it often arises in more serious situations. When it does it can be deadly. Perhaps that's why in the Old Testament God commanded the Jews not to put any yeast in their bread during seasons like Passover. He wanted to remind them that it can ruin the things that are most precious and holy.

It can contaminate our hearts, our lives, and ultimately our destiny.

If it's hard for you to wrap your mind around the idea that you have a destiny, think of it like my husband does. He says destiny is just a fancy word for destination, and we all have one of those. We're all on a path, going somewhere to do something. And if God has His way it will be something wonderful.

> For we are God's [own] handiwork (His workmanship), recreated in Christ Jesus, [born anew] that we may do those good works which God predestined (planned beforehand) for us [taking paths which He prepared ahead of time], that we should walk in them [living the good life which He prearranged and made ready for us to live]. Ephesians 2:10, AMP

We don't have to be ministers or missionaries to have a divine destiny. God has mapped out a mission for each one of us. He's called us all to do great, God-glorifying things. But to fulfill that call we must find out how to keep from being thrown off course when other people mistreat us. We must learn to keep a sharp eye out for yeast.

> We don't have to be ministers or missionaries to have a divine destiny. God has mapped out a mission for each one of us.

We can learn a lot about that from the heroes in the Bible (and we will in the following pages). But we can also take a few lessons from more recent history—from the lives of people like Benedict Arnold, for instance.

Ever heard of him?

You have if you've ever studied American history. He was the infamous traitor who betrayed his nation during the Revolutionary war. His name is so synonymous with betrayal that for years people have used his name as a byword, accusing disloyal friends of being "*Benedict Arnolds.*"

That's a terrible legacy! But here's the shocking truth: Benedict Arnold started out as a hero, as a man with a glorious destiny.

The facts of his life leave no doubt about it. In the early years of the revolutionary era his reputation for valor and brilliance on the battlefield rivaled that of George Washington's. He was admired throughout the colonies. He spent his own money to help finance the American cause and fought with such ferocity he earned the nickname "America's Hannibal."

As an officer in the Colonial Army, Benedict Arnold led his troops to seemingly impossible victories. The evidence of God's hand of protection upon him was undeniable: Horses were shot out from under him. Enemy fire ripped holes in his uniform and left him unscathed. When he did suffer life-threatening wounds, he survived against all odds and courageously rejoined the war.

> In the early years of the revolutionary era his reputation for valor and brilliance on the battlefield rivaled that of George Washington's.

But then the offenses came. Not petty ones. Not minor irritations. Real, heart-wrenching betrayals and injustices: A fellow officer stole the credit for one of his greatest military triumphs while Arnold, unable to set the record straight, lay helpless in the hospital. Then Congress compounded the insult by promoting five other officers—all Arnold's juniors—to higher ranks while ignoring his accomplishments and leaving his status unchanged.

Arnold made no secret of how such slights affected him. He wrote about them plainly in a letter to his friend and commander, General George Washington. "Having made every sacrifice of fortune and blood and become a cripple in the service of my country, I little expected to see the ungrateful returns I have received from my countrymen," he said.

No doubt, Washington could sympathize with Arnold's pain. He'd experienced it too. He suffered the same kinds of injustices from the very same people. While He poured out his life for his country, marshalling its forces with legendary excellence, his nation's leaders had repeatedly undermined him: They created a "Board of War," and staffed it with jealous politicians who over-ruled him at every turn. They refused him aid when he most needed it. They criticized him. They questioned his fitness to command. Some even called openly for his removal.

When you compare Washington's story to Arnold's, you have to ask: Why, after facing such similar mistreatment, did the two men turn out so differently?

This answer is simple. Arnold took the devil's bait.

He let his pain ferment into bitterness. He let it agitate him into acting like a fool. Determined to right the wrongs he'd suffered and reclaim the rewards he'd been denied, Benedict Arnold tripped the devil's trap-stick.

When he did, the cage fell. His destiny collapsed in ruins. So instead of finishing his race as a hero, he spent his dying days as a broken man and an exiled traitor. History records that he died with his war-worn Continental Army coat draped around his shoulders. "Let me die in this old uniform in which I fought my battles," he said as his life slipped away. "May God forgive me for wearing any other."

George Washington's story, of course, ended with far greater glory. But it could have been otherwise. Washington's legacy, too, could have been destroyed by Benedict Arnold. After all, Arnold was among his most trusted friends. Washington had believed in him and supported him for years. When Congress passed over Arnold for promotion, Washington came to his defense. He sent a letter of petition on Arnold's behalf. "Surely a more active, a more spirited and sensible officer fills no department in your army," he wrote.

Yet Arnold repaid his friend's faithfulness with treachery.

He used the position Washington had given him as commander over the fort at West Point to commit treason. When Washington received the news, those who delivered it reported that he wept over the betrayal as though his heart would break. "Whom can we trust now?" he cried.

Washington's faith in God could have suffered a mortal wound at that moment. That was the devil's clear intent. But General Washington didn't take the bait. He made that clear just a few months later. As he watched his troops file past him at Vails Gate, New York, he turned to a fellow patriot who had seen his anguish the day he'd gotten word about Arnold. "I know the answer to that question now," he said. "*Whom can we trust now?* The Invisible Hand...We can always trust in the Invisible Hand."

As a bit of history buff, I love that story. But even if history isn't your thing, these two men, these two destinies, are worth remembering because, as one author so aptly put it, they represent:

> One invaluable lesson for today: Always be on guard. It's easy to let seemingly mundane annoyances pile up until they boil over...Always be on guard. George Washington was; Benedict Arnold was not. One is now a national hero; one is now a national disgrace."[4]

When you think about it, that's really the lesson Jesus was teaching His disciples when He said, "Beware of the yeast of the Pharisees and Sadducees."

Be on guard.

Today more than ever we need to pay attention to that warning. We're living in a time when offense is on the increase. The traps of mistreatment are multiplying. The yeast that ferments emotions and corrupts destinies is on the rise.

It's not unexpected. The Bible said it would happen. Jesus told us that in the last days "you will hear of wars and rumors of wars... For nation will rise against nation, and kingdom against kingdom. And there will be famines, pestilences,

> Always be on guard. George Washington was; Benedict Arnold was not. One is now a national hero; one is now a national disgrace.

---
[4] Glenn Beck, *Being George Washington: The Indispensable Man* (New York: threshold Editions/Mercury Radio Arts, 2011)

and earthquakes in various places." (Sounds like the six o'clock news, doesn't it?) "And then many will be offended, will betray one another, and will hate one another." (Matthew 24:6, 7, 10, NKJV).

Many will be offended. It's a sad statement but it's true. In our day, many will stumble over the trap-stick. But you don't have to be among them. Instead, you can strip the devil of the one thing he depends on to make his traps effective: the element of surprise. You can uncover what he's up to and see exactly how to thwart his plan. Once you're equipped to counter his strategies with the wisdom of God's Word, you'll be able to keep on running even when others trip around you.

You'll be able to say with well-founded confidence, "No one will ever steal my destiny."

2

THE MAN WHO WOULD BE KING

[God] raised up David to be their king; of him He bore witness and said, I have found David son of Jesse a man after My own heart, who will do all My will and carry out My program fully.
Acts 13:22 AMP

Few people in the Bible can teach us more about navigating the minefields of mistreatment than David. He was betrayed more often and more savagely than most of us will ever be. Yet he not only survived, he thrived and fulfilled all the will of God.

Things could have turned out differently, though. If one wise woman hadn't stopped David from making the biggest mistake of his life, he might not be known today as the sweet psalmist of Israel. He might be remembered as the man who let a fool's mistreatment turn him into a mass murderer.

It's a startling thought, isn't it? Yet it almost happened. The man God destined and anointed to be the greatest Old Testament king who ever lived almost wrecked his dynasty—simply because an idiot named Nabal insulted him.

You may remember reading about the incident in the Bible. Maybe you even heard the story in church. Then again, maybe not. It doesn't find its way into sermons as often as the stories about, say, David and Goliath. But it's every bit as significant. Even though Goliath was a far more impressive villain than Nabal was, this is the blunt truth: Nabal came closer to conquering David than Goliath ever did.

On the face of it, such a statement sounds preposterous. After all, Goliath was a sword-swinging giant; Nabal was just a wealthy little weasel with a big mouth. But in David's life as in ours, the giants that fight us from the other side of the battlefield aren't always our biggest problem. Sometimes the greatest threats we face come from fellow soldiers and so-called "friendly fire." The real dangers arise when we're ambushed by someone on our own side.

> Sometimes the greatest threats we face come from fellow soldiers and so-called "friendly fire."

And that's where Nabal supposedly was—on David's side.

As an Israelite, he was David's fellow countryman. As a descendent of Caleb from David's own tribe of Judah, he was even a relative of sorts. He was also David's neighbor, the beneficiary of his kindness and aid. So his attack, though it involved no weapons, was up close and personal.

It also came at the worst possible time. During one of the most stressful seasons of David's life, when he had only one nerve left, Nabal decided to stomp on it.

* * *

At the time, David had already been putting up with mistreatment of one kind or another for years.

As a youngster, he suffered rejection at the hands of his father. Left out in the fields alone to tend the sheep, he wasn't even invited to the party when the prophet Samuel came to his house looking to anoint a new king. David's dad Jesse considered David unworthy even to be a candidate for such an honor.

When Samuel insisted on seeing David anyway and identified him as the Lord's chosen, David's brothers got jealous and rejected David too. From that point on, they wanted nothing to do with him. When he brought supplies to them and their fellow soldiers during the infamous battlefield standoff with Goliath, they didn't offer a single word of thanks. Instead, David's older brother Eliab got angry and accused him of having evil motives.

"What are you doing around here anyway?" he demanded. "What about those few sheep you're supposed to be taking care of? I know about your pride and dishonesty. You just want to see the battle!"[5] (David might have asked, "What battle?")

When David killed Goliath, things got even worse.

King Saul, envious of David's sudden popularity with the people, flew into an insane rage and decided to kill him. He and his troops tracked David like an animal, forcing him to flee to the wilderness. There David hid in caves with his ragtag militia and scavenged for food to survive. He literally spent years running for his life.

What had David done to deserve this kind of treatment?

Nothing at all. He'd become a target simply because he was called by God and anointed to be king. As a result, he learned early the lesson all us who are destined by God to "reign as kings in life"[6] must learn:

You don't become a king without a fight.

For years, David faced those fights without stumbling. He won them God's way. In the face of all the hurts, betrayals, rejections, and outright attacks, he kept the right attitude and refused to retaliate. He proved himself mightier than his persecutors by treating them with kindness.

Each time they provoked him and he responded with restraint, his self-discipline increased. He grew

---

[5] 1 Samuel 17:28
[6] Romans 5:17, AMP

stronger. One day that strength would put him on the throne of Israel. And David knew it. That's what kept him on the high road. It's what stopped him from being drawn into everybody else's petty issues.

He knew where he was headed and he didn't want to get off course. He had his sights set on fulfilling the plan of God.

For decades, David refused to let anything distract him from his divine purpose. He even passed up the perfect opportunity to avenge himself once and for all against King Saul. The chance presented itself one day when David was hiding in yet another cave and Saul, still in murderous pursuit, unwittingly chose to use that very same cave as an outhouse.

During those few vulnerable moments as Saul answered nature's call, David could have killed him with ease. He had plenty of encouragement to do it, too. "Now's your opportunity!" his men whispered. "Today is the day the LORD was talking about when he said, 'I will certainly put Saul into your power, to do with as you wish'" (1 Samuel 24:4).

> During those few vulnerable moments as Saul answered nature's call, David could have killed him with ease.

But, as always, David resisted the temptation. He decided to use his sword not to slay Saul but to prove his loyalty to him. He cut off a piece of Saul's robe without his knowledge and then followed him out of the cave shouting:

"My lord the king!...Why do you listen to the people who say I am trying to harm you? This very day you can see with your own eyes it isn't true...Look, my father, at what I have in my hand. It is a piece of your robe! I cut it off, but I didn't kill you. This proves that I am not trying to harm you and that I have not sinned against you, even though you have been hunting for me to kill me. The LORD will decide between us. Perhaps the LORD will punish you for what you are trying to do to me, but I will never harm you. As that old proverb says, 'From evil people come evil deeds.' So you can be sure I will never harm you" (vv. 8-13 NLT).

Look again at those last few verses. They reveal just how much David understood about the principles of God. He had a revelation that vengeance belongs to the Lord. He knew that if he took things into his own hands and struck out at Saul to even the score, he'd qualify as an 'evil man doing evil deeds.'

That's a great scriptural truth, and David had lived by it for many years. But he soon found out that no matter how well you know something, you can always let it slip. First Corinthians 10:12 says, "Let him who thinks he stands take heed lest he fall." And David, having just spoken those great words of revelation, was definitely headed for a fall.

YEAST CAN MAKE US DO DUMB STUFF

After taking the high road in the cave with Saul, David got back to the business of hiding out. He knew the king would try to kill him again. So he and his band of distressed, indebted, discontented men fled once more to a place in the wilderness called Maon.

The spot provided a temporary refuge. But even so, tensions in the camp were running high. In addition to Saul's threats, provisions had become a problem. David had a lot of mouths to feed. The Bible doesn't tell us exactly how many. But we do know that there were 600 men. Since men like the company of women, they probably had wives, and most likely a baby or two. That's a lot of groceries. All total, the group must have numbered well over a thousand.

Because they were living on the run, they couldn't settle down, plant crops, and raise livestock. So they stocked their pantries by raiding Philistine villages and stealing what they needed. In other words, they operated like a bunch of thieves. It sounds bad, I know. But there was some justice to it because the Philistines had been doing the same to the Israelites for years. They'd been attacking their herdsmen and stripping them of their flocks right and left.

Which brings us back to Nabal.

A wealthy Israelite from Maon who owned 3,000 sheep and 1,000 goats, he was a prime Philistine target. So when David moved into the neighborhood, he decided to do his kinsman a favor. He set up camp near Nabal's flocks and protected them from predators and thieves. He also gave stern warnings to any of his men who might be tempted to help themselves to an occasional sheep or goat: Nothing that belonged to Nabal would be touched.

Things went along fine for a while. Then one day David found himself in a bind. The Philistine cupboards had run bare and his clan was getting hungry. Figuring the logical thing to do was to ask for a return on his favor:

> When David heard that Nabal was shearing his sheep, he sent ten of his young men to Carmel. He told them to deliver this message: "Peace and prosperity to you, your family, and everything you own! I am told that you are shearing your sheep and goats. While your shepherds stayed among us near Carmel, we never harmed them, and nothing was ever stolen from them. Ask your own servants, and they will tell you this is true. So would you please be kind to us, since we have come at a time of celebration? Please give us any provisions you might have on hand" (1 Samuel 25:4-8).

This was a reasonable request. *Very* reasonable considering all that David had done for Nabal. There was just one problem: Nabal was not a reasonable man. He was a fool. In fact, that's the meaning of his name. The Bible describes him as rude, boorish, coarse, surly, snappish, and dishonest in all his dealings.

You'd think that kind of reputation, coupled with the name Fool, would have clued David in to the potential hazards of dealing with Nabal. But apparently David ignored the clues. He neglected to take the man's character into account and fell prey to unrealistic expectations.

We've all done that at one time or another. We've disregarded warning signs that should have alerted us to potential dangers posed by others. We've befriended the office critic, listened to him berate other employees, and then been surprised to find out that behind our back he was criticizing us too. We've put our trust in people even though they've already proven themselves to be untrustworthy.

> We've disregarded warning signs that should have alerted us to potential dangers posed by others.

When we operate with that kind of blind naiveté, we set ourselves up for offense. And that's exactly what David did. He set himself up to be shocked senseless by behavior that, coming from a greedy, cheating, disrespectful fool like Nabal, should have been utterly predictable. He let himself be blindsided by betrayal he would have seen coming if he'd used a little more wisdom.

Nabal answered David's servants saying:

> "Who is this fellow David?" Nabal sneered [when he heard David's request]. "Who does

this son of Jesse think he is? There are lots of servants these days who run away from their masters. Should I take my bread and water and the meat I've slaughtered for my shearers and give it to a band of outlaws who come from who knows where?" (vv. 10-11).

Nabal's response to David's request was an insulting slap in the face. It was also downright stupid. Why should Nabal take his food and give it to outlaws? Because they're outlaws, that's why! They're distraught, disgruntled, bankrupt, militant—and hungry! Refusing to feed them could be disastrous. Even a fool should have figured that out.

But Nabal was too busy dishing out dirt to David's messengers to consider such dangers. He was preoccupied with puffing himself up like a toad, pretending like he'd never even heard of David. It was a lie, of course. He knew full well who David was. Like everybody else in Israel, he'd heard about David's great victory against Goliath. He even knew the name of David's father. He also knew that David was a fugitive because of King Saul's murderous jealousy, not because he was a runaway slave.

These facts were all obvious to David the moment he heard what Nabal had said. So it's no wonder he was furious. But even so, if he hadn't added the yeast, he might have managed to escape the trap of offense. After all, he'd put up with far worse things than the rantings of a numskull like Nabal. He'd been rejected and insulted by his family. He'd been accused and slandered by his king. His own government had attempted to assassinate him. Yet, with godly self-control and even kindness, he'd endured it all.

David knew how to do this!

Why, then, would he let one surly, small-minded man get to him?

I don't know. Maybe he was hungry and his blood sugar was low. Maybe the attitude of his quick-tempered men had rubbed off on him. (The Bible does warn us, "Keep away from angry, short-tempered people, or you will learn to be like them and endanger your soul."[7]) Maybe the pressure of his circumstances had rubbed his emotions raw. Maybe he'd gotten so busy raiding Philistine villages that he'd neglected to spend time with the Great Shepherd of Psalm 23 who, in times past, had refreshed and restored his soul.

There's also another possibility.

Perhaps David thought the same thing we sometimes do in those situations: That Nabal was such a nobody, God wouldn't much care how David reacted toward him. Perhaps David felt that because he'd had been so long-suffering in the major areas of his life (with people of importance) he'd earned the right to blow his stack at this one, insignificant fool.

Whatever his reasoning or lack of it, David fell off the wagon of self-restraint. He let himself get agitated. He let his anger off the leash. Then he made a decision. Turning to his men he said, "Strap on your swords!"

---

[7] Proverbs 22:24-25

There's going to be a bloodbath tonight!" And David headed out with an army of 400 outlaws to get his revenge.

It was a rotten decision. But that's not surprising. We all make lousy decisions when we're boiling mad. Yeast-inflated emotions can cause us to do stupid stuff. Even though, like David, we're people after God's own heart; even though we have a divine calling, know the Bible, and have lived by it for years; when we react—whether in word or deed—out of irritation, pain, shock, or a feeling of betrayal, we do things that threaten our destiny.

> Whatever his reasoning or lack of it, David fell off the wagon of self-restraint. He let himself get agitated.

We don't realize it at the time, of course. Neither did David. Rage had pushed such thoughts out of his mind. As he marched with his men toward Nabal's house, vengeance burning in his eyes, he seemed like a different man than the one who had declared to Saul just a few days earlier that the Lord is the One who administers justice in such matters; He's the One who either punishes or repays.

Did David totally forget that revelation? Yes, it seems he did. His mind reeling from the mistreatment he'd suffered, all he cared about was getting even. And all he could do was complain.

"A lot of good it did to help this fellow," he said. "We protected his flocks in the wilderness, and nothing he owned was lost or stolen. But he has repaid me evil for good."[8]

Those statements were true, no question about it. It's not right to return evil for good. The Bible says so. But it also says that if you "Give freely without begrudging it...the LORD your God will bless you in everything you do."[9] He—*the Lord!*—will see to it that your "good deeds will never be forgotten."[10]

That's where David missed it. He made the assumption that because he'd done good deeds for Nabal, he had the right to expect repayment from him. But he was mistaken. He shouldn't have been looking for a return from Nabal, he should have been looking for a return from *God* because it's "from the Lord you will receive the reward..."[11]

As believers, we need to remember this principle. We need to keep in mind that although it's scriptural and right for us to expect a harvest on the seeds of blessing we sow into the lives of others, we get in trouble when we decide who should give us that harvest and how it should come. That's none of our business. It's God's deal. He said *He* would bring us the harvest. He said *He* would repay us and He'll do it however and through whomever He chooses.

---

[8] 1 Samuel 25:21
[9] Deuteronomy 15:10
[10] Psalms 112:9
[11] Colossians 3:24, NASB

"Well, even so, I resent it when a person I've gone out of my way to bless mistreats me," you might say. "And I think I have the right to complain about it!"

Yes, I suppose that's true. God gave you a free will, so if you choose to complain you can. But before you do it, you might want to consider the warning the Lord gave me a while back. He interrupted me one day when I was fussing about something and said, *If you complain, you will remain.*

I knew in an instant what He meant: Complaining keeps me stuck in the very situation I'm complaining about. It stops me from moving forward. It puts me in a state of stagnation. It stops the blessing of God from flowing.

Have you ever seen a pool of stagnant water? It can't go anywhere. All it can do is sit there stinking things up and attracting flies. I don't want to end up like that and I'm sure you don't either. So stop complaining. Whatever it is you're upset about, let it go! What difference does it make? God will take care of you.

He always takes care of us when we obey Him!

David should have focused on that fact instead of breathing out fire and brimstone against Nabal. He should have cooled himself down by recalling all the times God had been faithful to him through the years. Who knows what might have happened? He might have gotten caught up praising the Lord and forgotten about his hurt feelings. He might have turned around and gone home, dancing, singing, and rejoicing. And God would have met his need.

But David didn't do that. He kept complaining instead.

WAS THAT JUST EXTRA TESTOSTERONE TALKING?

The more David complained, the more he fanned the flame of his flesh. The more his flesh boiled up, the hotter his anger burned—proving that what James 3:4-6 says is true:

> The tongue is a small thing, but what enormous damage it can do. A tiny spark can set a great forest on fire. And the tongue is a flame of fire. It is full of wickedness that can ruin your whole life. It can turn the entire course of your life into a blazing flame of destruction, for it is set on fire by hell itself.

The Bible doesn't tell us everything David said but I think it's safe to assume he was just like the rest of us. Once he opened his mouth and started giving full expression to his anger, he just kept at it, building up steam. I imagine he said things like, "A lot of good it does

> The more David complained, the more he fanned the flame of his flesh. The more his flesh boiled up, the hotter his anger burned.

to help people out! Why did I even waste my time? I could have been feasting on lamb chops from that ingrate's flocks instead of standing guard over them. I'll give that maggot what he deserves!"

Although I can't confirm those specific statements with the Scriptures, the Bible does tell us this: After stewing for a while in his own anger, David eventually blurted out a statement that to a rational mind seems almost unthinkable. He said, "May God deal with me severely if even one man of his household is still alive tomorrow morning!"[12]

Excuse me? Was that just excess testosterone talking or did David seriously intend to kill every man in Nabal's house? Didn't he realize that would involve slaughtering people who'd done nothing wrong? That's not justice. It's mass murder! How could a man after God's own heart even consider committing such an atrocity?

I'll tell you how: His out-of-control emotions had distorted his judgment. That's what inflamed emotions always do. As Proverbs 14:29 warns, "Those who control their anger have great understanding; those with a hasty temper will make mistakes." Murder, especially the mass kind, is a BIG mistake. But David was about to make the biggest mistake of his life because he'd let his temper take over, and when any of us let our temper take over, we use more force to deal with situations than is necessary or right. Before we know it, we're hurting innocent people.

---

[12] 1 Samuel 25:22-23

Granted, most of us don't literally cut folks into pieces like David meant to do. We cut them up in more subtle ways. While we're standing in the department store line we work ourselves into lather over some injustice we've suffered and when the unsuspecting store clerk asks us a simple question we lash out at her.

"Would you like to apply for a Super Shopper credit card today?" she says.

"I say no to that question every week!" we snap back. "And the answer is still NO!" Then we storm off leaving the poor clerk close to tears.

Most of the time, we shrug off such incidents as insignificant. We assume they don't really matter. But the truth is they can matter a lot. Dennis and I were reminded of that early in our ministry during a trip to southern California. We'd gone to see a movie, something we don't often do. When we arrived at the theatre and tried to buy tickets, we couldn't understand what the woman behind the counter was saying. It sounded like she was asking, "General or lodge?" But she mumbled so much we really couldn't be sure.

Dennis asked her over and over, "What did you say?" and she continued to answer with the same indistinguishable mumble. Each time, his frustration increased. His voice got gruffer. His jaw got tighter. Finally, he told her with unmistakable aggravation that we just wanted "regular" seating, leaving it to her to figure out what that meant.

Sure enough, the tactic worked and she handed us the tickets. Then a look of recognition dawned on her face. "Hey, aren't you Dennis Burke?" she said. "You just preached at my church!"

Embarrassed and disappointed in ourselves, we learned a valuable lesson: you never know who's watching you. One lapse of self-control can wound a precious person who's looking at you hoping to see Jesus. One irritated outburst can rob you of priceless spiritual rewards. And it's never worth it. No matter how justified your anger may feel at the time, you'll always regret letting it off its tether. You'll always wish you'd reined it in with patience, kindness, and love.

> One lapse of self-control can wound a precious person who's looking at you hoping to see Jesus.

David was about to find that out the hard way. He was charging full speed ahead toward the worst kind of regret. The devil had set the trap for him. He'd baited it with feelings of shock, betrayal, and injustice; and David had taken the bait. He must have known somewhere in the depths of his heart that he was wrong. He must have realized he was taking a detour, stepping off the high road onto another path.

No doubt, he thought he had good reason; and I suppose he did. But then so do we all.

We all have reasons to be angry. We all have reasons to be bitter and resentful. We have reasons, yes, but we have no excuse because there is no excuse for sin. And yielding to offense, letting it dominate us and direct our decisions, allowing it to provoke us into violating God's law of love, is nothing short of sin.

In the end, sin always costs us more than we want to pay. But David wasn't thinking about the cost. He was too caught up in the violent storm of his own rage. He was so focused on destroying Nabal and his household that it never occurred to him he was about to destroy his own future as well.

That was the very thing the devil had been trying to trick David into doing all along. It's why he'd tempted David's kinfolks to throw him away like a dirty rag. It's why he'd incited Saul to hunt him down like a rabid dog. Satan wasn't just out to hurt David's feelings. He wasn't just trying to offend him. His goal was to overthrow the plan of God, defeat the man anointed to reign in righteousness over Israel, and stop him from fulfilling his destiny.

The devil has set his sights on doing the same thing to you. The reason is simple: He knows that you, as a born again child of Almighty God, are part of "a chosen race, a royal priesthood."[13] You're destined, through abundance of grace and of the gift of righteousness, to reign in life by...Jesus Christ."[14] In other words, just like David, you're anointed to be a king.

"But I thought Jesus is the King!" you might say.

He is. He's the King of Kings and the Lord of Lords. And, as believers, we're the kings He is King over. The Bible makes that clear. It says that Jesus has:

---

[13] 1 Peter 2:9, AMP
[14] Rom. 5:17, KJV

...loved us and washed us from our sins in His own blood, and has made us kings and priests to His God and Father, to Him be glory and dominion forever and ever. Amen. (Rev. 1:5-6 NKJV)

That's the good news.

The news that might not sound so good is this: Like David, you have to resist the devil at every turn if you want to fulfill your call. You have to deal with mistreatment from your own personal assortment of Jesses and Eliabs and Sauls. Every time you exercise restraint, every time you respond with patience and love, you'll grow stronger. And that strength will further equip you to reign in life.

If you've been a Christian for a while and you've been growing in the Lord, you've probably gained a lot of strength already. But always remember this: No matter how strong you become, no matter how many victories you win against your flesh, you'll still have to watch out for the Nabals. They're coming. You can count on it.

If you let them, they will get under your skin.

David can vouch for that.

3

THE WISE WOMAN AND THE FOOL

He that diggeth a pit shall fall into it; and whoso breaketh an hedge, a serpent shall bite him.
Ecclesiastes 10:8, KJV

It's never a good idea to tear down your hedge of divine protection. But during one of the most dangerous seasons of his life, that's exactly what David was planning to do. Never mind that he'd been living behind that hedge for years. Never mind that it was the only reason he was still alive. David was willing to cut a hole in it if that's what it took to even the score with Nabal.

You'd think David, of all people, would realize what a risk he was taking.

As the author of Psalm 91, he knew his safety was only guaranteed as long as he lived in the "shelter of the Most High." He understood that God promises supernatural protection, not to those who go charging out to avenge themselves but to those who say of the Lord: "He is my refuge and my fortress; My God, in Him I will trust."[15]

But it didn't matter. David's agitation had trumped every other truth. It had blinded him to the fact that by committing murder himself, David would open the door for Saul to murder him.

Ephesians 4:27 says, "Anger gives a mighty foothold to the Devil;"[16] and when the devil already has his guns turned in your direction, giving him any kind of foothold is a mighty dangerous thing to do. Good thing for David God had a back-up plan.

Her name was Abigail and she was Nabal's wife. According to the Bible, she was "a woman of good understanding and beautiful appearance."[17] She was, as one translation puts it, "sensible."[18] By definition that means she was levelheaded, wise, prudent, rational, reasonable, practical, and marked by good judgment.

Let me ask you something. When was the last time you heard somebody praised for being sensible or having good judgment? Can't remember, can you?

---

[15] Psalm 91:1-2
[16] Ephesians 4:27
[17] 1 Samuel 25:3
[18] Ibid, NLT

Such qualities don't get much press these days. They don't excite people because they aren't modeled by celebrities or applauded by the media. Tiara-crowned pageant winners don't stroll runways in sashes that read *Miss Sensible*. Starlets aren't chased down by paparazzi clamoring to photograph their good judgment.

Today as always, the world values outward appearance much more than character. Sad to say, believers often do too. Given the choice between sterling character and stunning good looks, any number of Christians would make the wrong choice. Their thinking colored by our contemporary culture, they believe—despite what the Bible says to the contrary—that beauty will take them farther in life than good sense.

Abigail, however, proved just the opposite. She showed us how much better our lives would be if we gave less attention to how we look and more to how we think.

"People judge by outward appearance, but the LORD looks at a person's thoughts and intentions."[19] And Abigail reveals why that's true. It wasn't her fetching face and form that saved David from disaster. It was the godly wisdom she'd learned to live by. It was her common sense—which, as we all know, isn't common at all.

Ralph Waldo Emerson once said that common sense is "as rare as genius;" and Abigail possessed one of the rarest of all revelations. She'd figured out how to

---

[19] 1 Samuel 16:7

deal with fools and the agitation they create without endangering her future.

That's something every one of us who wants to fulfill our destiny must learn. If we don't, fools will absolutely ruin us. They'll provoke us, agitate us, and mistreat us until we react and do something that will damage our destiny.

Personally, I've tried to learn everything I can from Abigail. I figure that living with Nabal was equivalent to earning a Master's Degree in managing fools. I must admit, however, that I used to wonder: Why, if she was so sensible, did she marry such a fool in the first place?

Then I remembered that in certain cultures marriages were arranged by parents. Since Nabal was rich, Abigail's parents probably decided he'd make a good husband. That turned out to be wrong, of course. But their daughter, having been wed to a jerk, made the best choice available to her. She set out to sweeten her life at every opportunity with the peace of God. She countered the toxic effect Nabal had on everyone around him and became an expert at making the most out of every situation.

She didn't wait to learn how to do it until David showed up with murder on his mind, either. Abigail worked on her peace-making skills for years. Early in her marriage, she witnessed Nabal's fiery interactions with others and realized, *One day this hothead is going to do something that could ruin us all. So I'd better get ready. I'd better arm myself with wisdom because someday I'm going to need it.*

As a result, Abigail was ready and knew what to do when one of Nabal's servants rushed in to tell her:

> David sent men from the wilderness to talk to our master, and he insulted them. But David's men were very good to us, and we never suffered any harm from them. Nothing was stolen from us the whole time they were with us. In fact, day and night they were like a wall of protection to us and the sheep. You'd better think fast, for there is going to be trouble for our master and his whole family. He's so ill-tempered that no one can even talk to him! (1 Samuel 25:14-17).

This was unusual information for a household servant to relay to someone in Abigail's position. Most servants in those days wouldn't dare say such things to the "lady of the house." They'd be afraid of being punished or accused of insubordination. But apparently, Abigail had banished such fears from her household. She needed allies in dealing with Nabal. So she'd established relationships between herself and the people who worked for her. She'd extended kindness to them and earned their trust.

It was a wise move.

It always is.

No matter what position of leadership we may occupy—whether at work, at church, or at home—we should always take the time to build relationships with the people around us. We should treat them with respect and love regardless of their pay grade or level of authority. Not only is it the godly thing to do, it's sensible too. If people know we care about them, they'll be more likely to guard our back when some fool tries to bring us down.

I always say, "Friends don't stand by watching while friends get slaughtered." If someone who's been faithful to me is about to be ambushed and I know it, I warn them in advance. If you're a faithful friend to others, they'll be apt to warn you too.

> If people know we care about them, they'll be more likely to guard our back when some fool tries to bring us down.

For Abigail, such a warning made all the difference. When she received it:

> Abigail lost no time. She quickly gathered two hundred loaves of bread, two skins of wine, five dressed sheep, nearly a bushel of roasted grain, one hundred raisin cakes, and two hundred fig cakes. She packed them on donkeys and said to her servants, "Go on ahead. I will follow you shortly." But she didn't tell her husband what she was doing (vv. 18-19).

I don't generally advocate sneaking around behind your husband's back, but in this case it was the only reasonable course of action. Abigail knew this from experience. She'd spent years studying Nabal. She'd acquainted herself with his character and mode of operation. Over the course of their marriage, she'd learned that when he acted the fool, she had three options: She could nag and try to change him; she could get mad and blame him; or she could do what's right.

Like most wives, she probably didn't always make the right choice when she first got married. (Nobody starts out with wisdom. It has to be gained over time.) As a newlywed, she might have tried nagging and blaming. She might have said, "You old fool! Look what you've done now! You better straighten up or we're all going to die!" But after a while she realized she couldn't talk any sense into him. He wasn't going to listen. Fools never do. As the Bible says:

- Pound on a fool all you like—you can't pound out foolishness (Proverbs 27:22 MSG).
- Don't waste your breath on fools, for they will despise the wisest advice (Proverbs 23:9).
- Fools have no interest in understanding; they only want to air their own opinions (Proverbs 18:2).

This is one reason Abigail qualified as a sensible woman: She took stock of Nabal's temperament and accepted it. She stopped trying to change him and just did what's right.

As simple as that sounds, most of us do the reverse. Instead of getting to know people and dealing with them in the light of who they are, we keep trying to make them who we want them to be. We keep banging on the same locked door even though it never opens. That makes life hard!

We could save ourselves so much trouble if we'd learn to mind our own business. It's not our job to go around convincing other people to do the right thing. We're not called to convict them when they're wrong. That job belongs to the Holy Spirit and we need to butt out and let Him do it. Think how much pressure that would take off of us! Most of us have been working ourselves silly trying to get our spouse, our parents, our siblings, our neighbors, and our fellow church members to behave like we think they should.

But their behavior isn't our responsibility!

When we stand before the judgment seat of Christ, "We will each receive whatever we deserve for the good or evil we have done in our bodies."[20] We'll each have to answer for our own choices. Jesus isn't going to ask us, "Who did you change? How successful were you at fixing your husband and your co-workers?" He's going to talk to us about ourselves and nobody else.

That's why He told us to stop worrying about the speck in our friend's eye, and deal instead with the log in our own![21] He wants us to stop obsessing over

---

[20] 2 Corinthians 5:10
[21] See Matthew 7:3

other people's deficiencies and concentrate on our own personal growth. If we'll do that, it will not only serve us well in the hereafter, it will cut down on a lot of aggravation in the here and now.

SAVING TWO CAUSES WITH ONE SPEECH

Actually, if Abigail hadn't learned to stop fretting about other people's behavior, she would have been doubly ticked off by this situation. She would have been offended not just at her husband but at David too. After all, he had threatened her whole family with annihilation when nobody but Nabal had done anything wrong. He'd allowed a fool's foolishness to spark his anger and now she had to risk her own neck to stop him from taking revenge.

Abigail had every reason to be mad. But she refused to go there. It would only make matters worse and she knew it. "A wise woman builds her house; a foolish woman tears hers down with her own hands"[22] and Abigail was one wise woman. Determined not to further endanger her family, she kept her attention on the greater cause: Saving the lives of the people she loved.

Her strategy was simple. First, she sent her servants ahead of her with grocery-laden donkeys to meet David and his blood-thirsty men on the road. (Maybe she hoped some appetizers would lighten their mood.) Then she headed out to meet David herself. On the way, she considered what she should say. It occurred to

---
[22] Proverbs 14:1

her that just as she had a household to save, David had a future as king. He too had a greater cause. He'd just lost sight of it during the encounter with Nabal.

Women tend to be skilled multi-taskers, so Abigail hit on a brilliant solution: By reminding David of his destiny, she could protect her family and preserve his royal dynasty at the same time. She could save two causes with one speech.

* * *

I can only imagine what David thought when he saw her riding toward him, trailing clouds of dust as she spurred her donkey to a run. This wasn't part of his plan! He was looking for a bloodbath not a woman! What could she possibly want?

He didn't have to wait long to find out.

> When Abigail saw David, she quickly got off her donkey and bowed low before him. She fell at his feet and said, 'I accept all blame in this matter, my lord. Please listen to what I have to say. I know Nabal is a wicked and ill-tempered man; please don't pay any attention to him. He is a fool, just as his name suggests. But I never even saw the messengers you sent. Now, my lord, as surely as the LORD lives and you yourself live, since the LORD has kept you from murdering and taking vengeance into your own hands, let all your enemies be as cursed as Nabal is. And here is a present I have brought

to you and your young men. Please forgive me if I have offended you in any way' (1 Samuel 25:24-28).

Look again at the first and last words Abigail said: *I accept all blame...Please forgive me if I have offended you.* Unusual words, aren't they? It's rare these days to hear somebody take the blame even when they're at fault, much less when they're innocent. Most people would never ask forgiveness for something they didn't do. "I can't just be a wimp and let people walk all over me," they'd say. "That would make me a doormat!"

Abigail, however, knew better. The trouble Nabal caused wasn't her first rodeo. She'd been in such situations many times before. She'd learned by experience that humbling herself to make peace was anything but wimpish. It required strength, courage, and self-control.

She'd also witnessed firsthand how arguments escalated when everybody involved insisted they were right. This time she couldn't afford to let that happen. Her blockheaded husband had put the lives of everybody in the household on the line. This was a matter of life or death.

Abigail didn't care who was right and who was wrong. She cared about her future and her family surviving to see another day. So, putting aside her fleshly pride, she humbled herself and did what was necessary to stop the strife.

If you and I value our destiny, we'll do the same. We'll take the blame even for situations that aren't our fault. We'll apologize and ask forgiveness even if we're not the one who was wrong. Reasoning things out like Abigail did, we'll come to the same conclusion: What does it matter who's right if we're dead?

"Oh, Vikki, you're exaggerating," you might say. "Nobody is coming to kill me. That was Abigail's problem not mine."

On the contrary, my friend. The devil is out to kill all of us. He'll use any opportunity we give him to do it. And since "where...strife is, there is confusion and every evil work,"[23] we can't afford to engage in it.

At all.

Ever.

For any reason.

I realize that may sound extreme but this is serious business. When we get in strife with somebody, we open the door to the devil. We usher him into our lives and give him permission to do whatever he wants. In case you haven't already figured it out,

> Abigail didn't care who was right and who was wrong. She cared about her future and her family surviving to see another day.

he's a mean devil. He hates everything about you. His purpose is to steal, kill, and destroy your family, your health, your finances, and your future. He's ruthless.

Are you really willing to give the devil access to you just so you can get the last word in an argument? Do

---
[23] James 3:16 KJV

you really want to let him into your life just so you can prove you're right and tell somebody off? Of course not! Me either. Yet sometimes, when we let our flesh get the best of us, we do it anyway.

No wonder Romans 8:13 says, "The best thing you can do for your flesh is give it a decent burial and get on with your new life."[24] Our flesh will get us in trouble! It doesn't seek the things of God.

So we have to die to the flesh. And once we realize our destiny is at stake, that's easier for us to do.

Abigail took that fact into account when she approached David. She knew he'd be more likely to over-ride his anger if he realized his own destiny was at stake. So she made a point of re-awakening him to his divine calling. She helped him realize he was risking his God-ordained future for something of no value at all.

Bowing in humility at his feet, this is what she said:

> Please forgive me if I have offended in any way. The LORD will surely reward you with a lasting dynasty, for you are fighting the Lord's battles. And you have not done wrong throughout your entire life. Even when you are chased by those who seek your life, you are safe in the care of the LORD your God, secure in his treasure pouch! But the lives of your enemies will disappear like stones shot from a sling! When the LORD has done all he promised

---
[24] Message

and has made you leader of Israel, don't let this be a blemish on your record. Then you won't have to carry on your conscience the staggering burden of needless bloodshed and vengeance. And when the LORD has done these great things for you, please remember me! (1 Samuel 25:28-31).

Reading Abigail's words, you might wonder where she got all this revelation. How did she know David had maintained the moral high ground when King Saul had attacked him? What made her so sure he'd be the leader of Israel—a king with a "lasting dynasty?"

Some commentaries have suggested she had a prophetic edge because she'd grown up in the vicinity of the Old Testament school of the prophets. That may be true, I don't know. But there's another, even stronger possibility: The entire nation of Israel knew these things. They'd heard about David—about his courage in battle and his dependence on God to protect him. For years, the fierce words of faith he'd spoken to Goliath had been passed along from one person to another:

> You come to me with sword, spear, and javelin, but I come to you in the name of the LORD Almighty—the God of the armies of Israel, whom you have defied. Today the LORD will conquer you, and I will kill you and cut off your head....and the whole world will know that there is a God in Israel! And

everyone will know that the LORD does not need weapons to rescue his people. It is his battle, not ours. The LORD will give you to us! (1 Samuel 17:45-47).

Ever since the day David made that declaration the whole nation had been watching him with hope. Ever since the crowds had lined the roadside to celebrate when he marched back home in triumph with Goliath's head in his hand, they'd been thinking, *At last the Lord has sent us His anointed! He's raising up a king who truly believes, a king who will put on display the virtue, principles, and power of Almighty God!*

Most likely, that's what Abigail was thinking too. Just like the other Israelites of her day, she'd been waiting for years to see David's future unfold. She knew who he was destined to be.

David, however, had forgotten. Living in obscurity in the wilderness, pilfering Philistine pantries to put food on the table, he didn't think anyone was watching anymore. Abigail reminded him they were.

I've already said this, but it's a point worth repeating: They're watching you and me too. People all around us are hoping to see in us a living expression of the Most High God. Like the multitudes who thronged the shores of the Galilee a couple of thousand years ago, they're waiting to see Jesus in us.

When they do, they'll flock to Him in droves to receive Him as Lord of their lives.

Could such a thing really happen? you might wonder. *Can Christians like us really manifest Jesus in a way that will draw a lost world to Him?*

Yes we can...and we will when we start following the example of Abigail: remembering every moment of every day that we're living for a greater cause; refusing to let mistreatment of any kind, big or small, distract us from our mission.

> People all around us are hoping to see in us a living expression of the Most High God.

It won't be easy, that's for certain. As long as we live in this mortal body our flesh will try to fight us. Even though we've buried it by faith, it will pop up out of its spiritual coffin on a regular basis and we'll have to put it back in again. What's more, this side of heaven, we'll always have the devil to deal with. He's constantly trying to convince us we're nobody special. That we have no greater cause; no God-ordained destiny. That we're just ordinary people living ordinary lives.

We can be tempted at times to believe it, too, because our days often look a lot like David's did in the wilderness. Busy with the mundane things of life, we go to work, tend to the kids, clean house, and put food on the table. We don't feel like we're living in a supernatural spotlight putting Jesus on display for the world to see.

As a result, we can make the same miscalculation David did. We can conclude that no one is looking at us anymore and give in to our flesh. We can forget we're on a divine course and make some stupid move that sets us on a detour.

What's so bad about detours?

They cause us to miss God-ordained assignments. They cheat us out of precious earthly and heavenly rewards. They rob us of moments of divine destiny.

I saw a few years ago how easily that can happen. We were on motorcycle trip with some friends when we ran into a situation that seemed so ordinary (and irritating) that we would have never guessed it was a divine appointment.

> What's so bad about detours? They cause us to miss God-ordained assignments. They rob us of moments of divine destiny.

We stopped to have lunch at a restaurant and encountered a waitress who was downright rude. When we asked her for something she all but ignored us. If we repeated our request, she bristled with hostility. Her attitude annoyed all of us and we could have easily justified reporting her to the manager. But one member of our group—my friend Gloria—remembered the greater cause.

"Our waitress must be having a bad day," she said. (I thought that was an understatement.) "Let's be especially kind to her and help her day turn around."

The rest of us agreed and got on board. Every time the waitress came to the table, we went out of our way to say something nice to her. When she neglected to refill our water glasses or forgot to bring what we had requested, we responded with understanding. We stopped making any more demands and just looked for ways to encourage her.

At the end of the meal, her story came out. Someone she loved had been in a terrible accident. After her shift she would be leaving to drive several hours to the hospital. We asked if we could pray with her. She said yes. So we got the opportunity to bring the anointing of God into the situation, and share the love of Jesus with that waitress at a crucial moment in her life. When we left the restaurant, she waved us goodbye, brimming with gratitude.

Now *that's* what I call a victory: We went on our way rejoicing. A door was opened for God to pour out His glory in greater measure. And, most important of all, the waitress was blessed. I doubt if she'll ever forget the love we showed her that day. But even if she did, the Lord never will. He always remembers the good we do. He always rewards us in His own good time and His own good way.

Looking back now, I'm so glad Gloria reminded us of our greater cause! What if she hadn't? Or what if the rest of us had decided we were too famished and road-weary to do what she suggested? We might have missed out on what God had planned. We might have yielded to our irritation, taken a detour, and let the devil devour a portion of our destiny.

That's what would have happened to David if he hadn't listened to Abigail. He would have broken the heart and the hope of a nation. He would have put a blemish on his record that he would have regretted forever. But, thank God, that's not how the story ends. Instead:

> David replied to Abigail, "Praise the LORD, the God of Israel, who has sent you to meet me today! Thank God for your good sense! Bless you for keeping me from murdering the man and carrying out vengeance with my own hands. For I swear by the LORD, the God of Israel, who has kept me from hurting you, that if you had not hurried out to meet me, not one of Nabal's men would be alive tomorrow morning." Then David accepted her gifts and told her, "Return home in peace. We will not kill your husband" (1 Samuel 25:32-35).

It can sometimes be irritating to receive the kind of correction Abigail gave David—even if it's offered in a humble, loving way. We don't always want to hear the calming counsel of another believer (or even the Word of God) when our heart is stinging with the pain of mistreatment and our pulse is racing with rage. We'd rather close our ears and say, "Leave me alone! You don't know how I feel!" We'd rather do things our own way.

But if we value our destiny, we'll over-ride that reaction. We'll pay attention to the people God sends to help us. We'll heed the guidance He gave in Proverbs 15:31: "He whose ear listens to the life-giving reproof will dwell among the wise."[25]

David chose to receive that counsel. He listened to Abigail's reproof. As a result he will forever be known, not as a self-avenging, mass murderer, but as:

David, the man to whom God gave such wonderful success, David, the man anointed by the God of Jacob, David, the sweet psalmist of Israel. A man about whom God said, "David...is a man after my own heart, for he will do everything I want him to" (2 Samuel 23:1; Acts 13:22).

"But what about that rascal Nabal?" you might ask. "Did he ever get what was coming to him?"

Yes, he did. But not at David's hand.

Not at Abigail's either. A wise, peace-loving woman to the end, she didn't even shake a scolding finger in her husband's face after she saved him and the rest of the household from slaughter. She didn't rush right in and say, "You fool, let me tell you what almost happened today!" No...

> When Abigail arrived home, she found that Nabal had thrown a big party and was celebrating like a king. He was very drunk, so she didn't tell him anything about her meeting with David until the next morning. The next morning when he was sober, she told him what had happened. As a result he had a stroke, and he lay

---

[25] NASB

on his bed paralyzed. About ten days later, the LORD struck him and he died. When David heard that Nabal was dead, he said, "Praise the LORD, who has paid back Nabal and kept me from doing it myself. Nabal has received the punishment for his sin." Then David wasted no time in sending messengers to Abigail to ask her to become his wife (1 Samuel 25:36-39).

So ends the incident of the wise woman, the fool, and the man who would be king. Each one of them finished their earthly story long ago. But you and I are still here, living ours out. We still have decisions to make. We still have the opportunity to choose how we'll respond when somebody does us wrong. Let's remember our greater cause, heed the wise woman's counsel, and live like the kings God has called us to be.

4

NEVER!

It is not an enemy who taunts me—I could bear that. It is not my foes who so arrogantly insult me—I could have hidden from them. Instead, it is you—my equal, my companion and close friend.
Psalm 55:12-13

Taking the high road would be easier if life were more like Star Wars. Or at least like the Star Wars show at the Jedi Academy at Disneyland. The battle between good and evil is obvious there. Making the right choice is so simple that even a four year-old can do it.

Ask my grandson Jude. He knows. An enormous Star Wars fan, he got to be a part of the Disneyland show a few years ago during a family vacation. My daughter had prayed in advance that he'd be one of the kids selected from the audience to participate. (She's such a good mom!) Her prayer was answered when Jude was picked to play the character of his dreams: a Jedi-in-training.

Within seconds, he donned the identity of a little Luke Skywalker. He jumped with enthusiasm into his part and at the end of the show received his official Jedi Master Certificate. Then suddenly, at his moment of triumph, something shocking happened.

Darth Vadar's evil voice filled the room.

"Come to the Dark Side…" it beckoned.

Jude's eyes widened at the sound. He stiffened his stance against the sinister invitation. But he didn't miss a beat. He growled out his answer in a voice fierce with resolve. "NEVER!" he said. Then, to everyone's surprise, he charged forward with his light saber, ready to fight.

Ever since then, Jude's reply has become a favorite in our household. Dennis and I use it all the time. Whenever somebody's behavior tempts us to give in to the Dark Side, we growl just like Jude did. *"NEVER!"*

> Darth Vadar's evil voice filled the room "Come to the Dark Side." Jude growled out his answer in a voice fierce with resolve: "NEVER!"

It not only makes us laugh—a wise thing to do when the yeast of agitation starts rising—it also reminds us of some very serious, scriptural instructions:

NEVER pay back a bad turn with a bad turn or an insult with another insult, but on the contrary pay back with good... [*NEVER*] retaliate when people say unkind things about you. Instead, pay them back with a blessing. That is what God wants you to do, and he will bless you for it (See 1 Peter 3:9 Phillips, NLT).

Never is a strong word. It means *not ever, at no time, not at all, absolutely not, to no extent or degree*. And it's the word we need to remember when somebody does us wrong.

Like a glaring, red stop sign, *NEVER!* can bring us to a screeching halt when we're about to deal back to somebody a little of the hurt they've caused us. It can cool us down when we're about to boil over and put them in their place. It can warm us up when we're about to give them the cold shoulder.

NEVER! will remind us that even seemingly small retributions are contrary to God's command. He doesn't distinguish between major and minor "bad turns." He lumps all of them into one category and instructs us to pay them all back with good. Any suggestion to do otherwise comes from the great villain of the universe. And there is only one acceptable response.

NEVER!

"Oh, please! You can't be serious!" somebody might say. "Do you mean I can't even be catty to the backstabbing gossips at the office and the relatives who swindled me out of my inheritance? I'm not supposed to get back at them in any way?"

Not ever, at no time, not at all, absolutely not, to no extent or degree.

"But that's not fair! Why would God put those kinds of restraints on me?"

Because He wants to protect you. He wants you to be blessed, and He knows that even a trivial act of revenge will lead you out of the land of blessing and onto the dark side. It will set you on a slippery slope that will put your very destiny in danger.

What's worse, you won't even realize what's happening. Real life isn't like the Jedi Academy. When the devil beckons us onto his territory, he doesn't announce himself like Darth Vader at Disneyland. If he did, we'd go after him with light sabers blazing. So he employs another M.O. He masquerades as our ally. He pets our hurt feelings. He tells us our resentment is justified and a little bit of vengeance is appropriate, even right.

It's a toxic bunch of lies but the devil has been selling it to God's people with surprising success for thousands of years. Untold numbers have bought into it big time. One of them, an Old Testament Israelite named Ahithophel, paid an especially high price for it. Before we get fooled into doing the same, we might want to consider what happened to him.

SEX, LIES, MURDER...AND REVENGE

If anybody ever had good reasons for revenge, Ahithophel did. He saw his family dishonored, one member violated and another murdered. All by one of his closest friends.

The friend's name was King David.

The family members that David betrayed were Ahithophel's granddaughter Bathsheba and her husband Uriah.

The scandal of David and Bathsheba is among the most notorious in history. It happened, as the Bible says, "one spring, at the time of year when kings go to war." David had decided to stay at home in Jerusalem instead of going out to fight with his troops. Unable to sleep one night, he'd gone for a walk on the roof of his house...

> And from the roof he saw a woman bathing, and the woman was very beautiful to behold. So David sent and inquired about the woman. And someone said, "Is this not Bathsheba, the daughter of Eliam, the wife of Uriah the Hittite?" Then David sent messengers, and took her; and she came to him, and he lay with her... (2 Samuel 11:1-4).

When Bathsheba ended up pregnant as a result of the encounter, David did something even worse. He arranged for her husband to be killed while on the battlefield fighting for Israel. Then David married Bathsheba, thinking he'd covered up his sin.

He hadn't, of course. God had seen everything and He sent the prophet Nathan to confront David about it. Mortified, David repented in tears and agony. God forgave him. And though David and Bathsheba's baby died, they were able to go on with their lives. They conceived another child named Solomon who became Israel's next, great king.

As modern day believers most of us like the way that story ends. We're glad God is merciful and forgiving. We celebrate the fact that even a situation as reprehensible as David and Bathsheba's can be redeemed.

But Ahithophel didn't see it that way. He took David's sin more personally than we do.

It's easy to understand why. As one of David's most trusted advisors, Ahithophel had worked with him for years. They'd worshipped together in the tabernacle. Ahithophel even built his home in the shadow of the palace. He and his king weren't just associates. They were confidantes, companions, and friends.

David had known full well when he learned of Bathsheba's identity that she was Ahithophel's granddaughter. Yet he'd sent for her anyway. He'd used his power as king to abuse and betray Ahithophel's trust.

> We celebrate the fact that a situation as reprehensible as David and Bathsheba's can be redeemed. But Ahithophel didn't see it that way.

Let me stop here for a moment and assure you: God does not condone abuse of any kind and He doesn't require His people to do so either. He gives us guidance in His Word about how to protect ourselves from it. He teaches us what actions to take when we encounter it and how to process the pain it has caused us. We'll talk a lot about that in the upcoming chapters. But for now I want to make it clear that taking the high road doesn't mean you permit people to continually abuse you.

That wasn't Ahithophel's situation. Although he was wronged by David, it was a one-time event. David repented. He tried to make things right for Bathsheba and never committed that sin again.

The Bible doesn't say whether or not Ahithophel knew about David's repentance. Perhaps he didn't. It's possible that only Nathan and God Himself were privy to the king's gut-wrenching grief over what he'd done. So Ahithophel might have assumed the violation of his granddaughter had just been ignored.

If so, he was dead wrong. But then, that's one of the problems with judging other people and taking justice into our hands, isn't it? We never really know all the facts. We can wind up condemning someone for a sin God has already forgiven. That's a dangerous mistake, and Ahithophel made it. He decided David should be punished and waited in bitterness for years for the chance to make David pay.

The opportunity presented itself in the form of David's son Absalom. Like Ahithophel, he too had good reasons to want revenge. His sister Tamar had been raped by his half brother Amnon, and their father had done nothing about it.

David could have restored Tamar's honor. He could have exerted his authority as patriarch and king and demanded that Amnon marry her. But he didn't. He looked the other way. He allowed Tamar to be shamed and rejected. So Absalom took matters into his own hands. He had Amnon killed.

When David heard what had happened, he showed Absalom no mercy. He banished him from the palace and resolved never to see him again.

To say David handled the situation badly doesn't even begin to cover it. He wronged Tamar by refusing her the justice she deserved. He wronged Amnon by failing to hold him accountable for his actions. He wronged Absalom by leaving him to handle the fallout. Then, when the situation ended in murder, David reacted as if he, himself, was completely free of blame.

If you ever need proof that good people—people who are anointed by God to occupy important places in your life—can do wrong things, remember David and the way he mistreated Ahithophel and Absalom. He made some colossal blunders in his relationships with them. He hurt them in significant ways.

As usual, the devil exploited those failures. He convinced Absalom and Ahithophel that David was an enemy and encouraged them to treat him like one. So, as bitter people tend to do, they put their heads together and came up with their own brand of justice.

IF YOU'RE SITTING IN THE JUDGMENT SEAT OF CHRIST, YOU'RE IN THE WRONG CHAIR

Hebrews 12:15 says a root of bitterness "grows up to cause trouble and defile many." Absalom lived out that truth. He drew literally thousands of people into his web of offense.

> He got up early every morning and went out to the gate of the city. When people brought a case to the king for judgment, Absalom would ask where they were from, and they would tell him their tribe. Then Absalom would say, "You've really got a strong case here! It's too bad the king doesn't have anyone to hear it. I wish I were the judge. Then people could bring their problems to me, and I would give them justice!" (2 Samuel 15:2-4).

Once the seeds of discontent had been planted, Absalom incited a rebellion in Israel. He crowned himself king. He commandeered Israel's army. He forced his father's forces to flee Jerusalem. Then he called on Ahithophel to devise a plan that would wipe out David once and for all.

Ahithophel's plan would have insured Absalom's victory...if it hadn't been for one man. *Hushai*. He was also a friend of David's who pretended to be part of the rebellion. When Absalom asked Hushai's opinion of Ahithophel's advice, Hushai said, "This time I think Ahithophel has made a mistake."[26] Then he suggested a strategy that was certain to fail.

Amazingly enough, Absalom fell for it. He and all the leaders of Israel said, "Hushai's advice is better than Ahithophel's.' For the LORD had arranged to defeat

---
[26] 2 Samuel 17:7

the counsel of Ahithophel, which really was the better plan, so that he could bring disaster upon Absalom!"[27]

To be clear, God didn't really want to destroy Absalom. He had good plans for him. He'd designed a royal destiny for him to fulfill. As David's son, Absalom was a potential heir to the throne. He was a prince of Israel who could have fought at his father's side, won battles, been memorialized in Scripture, and received eternal rewards. But he chose another path. He listened to the tempter's voice and defected to the dark side, pitting himself not just against David but against God.

> Absalom could have fought at his father's side, but he chose another path. He listened to the tempter's voice and defected to the dark side.

Fighting God is always a losing proposition. It's also the dumbest thing anybody can do.

What was Absalom thinking?

The same thing we often do in such situations. He thought he was right. He thought he was ridding Israel of an unjust king and offering people a better alternative. Isn't that the mindset we all have when we go after one of God's people who've done us wrong? As we make the rounds telling everybody how they mistreated us, don't we like to think we're protecting folks and doing them a favor?

---
[27] Verse 14

Sure we do. But that's not how God thinks about it. The way He sees it, we're siding against Him when we pass judgment on His people.

"But what if they deserve that judgment?" you might ask.

I'll let the Apostle Paul answer that question. He said:

> Who are you to judge another's servant? To his own master he stands or falls...Therefore do not go on passing judgment before the time, but wait until the Lord comes who will both bring to light the things hidden in the darkness and disclose the motives of men's hearts; and then each man's praise will come to him from God.[28]

In other words, only God knows what people deserve. So we need to stop worrying about it, get off the Judgment Seat of Christ, and let Him sort it out.

Absalom didn't do that. Instead, he let his pain and anger drive him to become both a judge and an executioner. Falling for one of the devil's favorite deceptions, he decided that justice would be served and his own future preserved by bringing David down.

> Only God knows what people deserve. So we need to stop worrying about it, get off the Judgment Seat of Christ, and let Him sort it out.

---
[28] Romans 14:4, 1 Corinthians 4:5, NASB

We all buy that lie at one time or another. When someone hurts us and tries to hinder our advancement, we think we have to fight them to protect God's plan for our lives. But that's just not true. As long as we stay on God's side, trusting and obeying Him, no one can steal our destiny.

God has guaranteed it. He has given us His Word: "No weapon turned against you will succeed."[29]

That's a powerful promise and it cuts like a sword. If you're on the right side, it protects you. If you're on the wrong side, it can destroy you.

Absalom chose the wrong side. As a result, he fell for Hushai's ruse and approved the wrong plan. Ahithophel knew the moment it happened that the rebellion was doomed. So, having been stripped of his honor, his reputation, and his future in the king's court, "he saddled his donkey, went to his hometown, set his affairs in order, and hanged himself."[30]

Not long afterward, Absalom died too. He was trying to escape King David's forces when he rode his mule under an oak tree and his hair got tangled in the branches. "His mule kept going and left him dangling in the air...Then [Joab, David's general] took three daggers and plunged them into Absalom's heart as he dangled from the oak still alive. Ten of Joab's young armor bearers then surrounded Absalom and killed him."[31]

---

[29] Isaiah 54:17
[30] 2 Samuel 17:23
[31] 2 Samuel 18:9, 14-15

It was a tragic death for the son of the king. But here's the saddest part: Absalom wasn't the only man who sacrificed his destiny on the altar of offense that day. The bitterness he'd sown infected Israel's entire army.

> So the battle began in the forest of Ephraim, and the Israelite troops were beaten back by David's men. There was a great slaughter, and twenty thousand men laid down their lives...[32]

Imagine, 20,000 dead. All because two people stepped onto the slippery slope that leads to the dark side.

WHAT OTHER CHOICE DID THEY HAVE?

It's easy for us, as contemporary believers, to throw stones at Absalom and Ahithophel for their attack against David. But if we put ourselves in their place, we have to wonder: What were they supposed to do? Pretend they hadn't been wounded by the way he'd treated them and their loved ones? Shrug their shoulders and say their pain didn't matter?

No.

They had another option available to them. They could have taken the road that David chose.

You have to remember, David was hurting too. His own son had plotted to kill him and steal his crown. He'd been blindsided by the worst kind of betrayal. Although his relationship with Absalom had been

---
[32] Verses 6-7

rocky in the past, David had ended their estrangement four years earlier. He'd brought his son back to the palace. Their fellowship had been restored. David loved Absalom dearly and assumed his son loved him too.

As for Ahithophel, David had no idea he was still angry over what had happened with Bathsheba. That sin was in the past. David thought he and his friend had put it behind them. Taking Ahithophel's pretense of loyalty at face value, he never suspected his closest counselor was playing him for a fool.

"It is not an enemy who taunts me," he wrote in Psalm 55, "I could bear that..."

> It is not my foes who so arrogantly insult me—I could have hidden from them. Instead, it is you—my equal, my companion and close friend. What good fellowship we enjoyed as we walked together to the house of God... As for this friend of mine, he betrayed me; he broke his promises. His words are as smooth as cream, but in his heart is war. His words are as soothing as lotion, but underneath are daggers! (vv. 12-14, 20-21).

No question about it, the treachery of David's family and friends left him reeling. So what did he do? How did he process his nightmarish pain?

He prayed.

That's right. Psalm 55 is a prayer.

When you read it you can see that David didn't deny the emotions he was feeling. But he didn't let them drive him to take matters into his own hands and retaliate either. Instead he dumped the entire mess into the lap of God.

You and I can do that too. When the pain of mistreatment starts pushing us toward offense, we can run to the Lord and He'll help us. He will give us "more and more grace."[33]

The same could have been true for Absalom and Ahithophel. If they'd talked to God about their anger toward David, God would have helped them handle it. He would have strengthened them and shown them what to do. But they didn't ask for His help. Maybe they had the misconception—like a lot of Christians do these days—that God only listens to prayers that are pretty and polite. Maybe they thought He'd strike them with lightning if they just opened up and spilled their guts.

One thing's for sure, David didn't have those misconceptions. He told the straight story when he prayed; and he told it directly to God. He didn't run around to all his friends sobbing on their shoulder. He didn't drag everybody else into the mud with him. He knew that wouldn't solve the problem. It would only make things worse. If he burdened other people with the details of how he'd been betrayed, they'd get upset too. The mess would get bigger instead of smaller.

So David limited himself to an audience of One.

---
[33] James 4:6, AMP

Confident the Almighty could handle his turbulent emotions, he poured them out with passion and said:

> Listen to my prayer, O God. Do not ignore my cry for help! Please listen and answer me, for I am overwhelmed by my troubles. My enemies shout at me, making loud and wicked threats. They bring trouble on me, hunting me down in their anger. My heart is in anguish. The terror of death overpowers me. Fear and trembling overwhelm me. I can't stop shaking. Oh, how I wish I had wings like a dove; then I would fly away and rest! I would fly far away to the quiet of the wilderness...How quickly I would escape—far away from this wild storm of hatred.[34]

David minced no words in telling God how torn up he was about the wrongs he had suffered. He was specific. He was graphic. He was emotional. Not because God needed the information but because he needed to express his feelings to Someone—the only One in the universe—who could do something about them.

No Counselor on earth can compare to God.

Certainly Christian therapists can provide valuable help now and then. They can be a great blessing to us as believers. During one of the most difficult times in my life, the Lord led me to seek out a counselor's help and I'll always be grateful for the input she gave me. But there's no one who can do for us what God can do.

---

[34] Psalm 55:1-8

He will not only heal our wounded heart when injustice threatens to destroy us; He will defend us and make things right.

David understood that. So as he prayed, his faith began to surge. "The LORD hears my voice!" he said. "He rescues me and keeps me safe from the battle waged against me, even though many still oppose me. God, who is king forever, will hear me and...save me."[35]

> David minced no words in telling God how torn up he was about the wrongs he had suffered. He was specific. He was graphic. He was emotional.

PULLING MOSES OFF HIS HIGH HORSE

David is a major scriptural hero so we might assume that God heard his prayer and saved him from his enemies because he was...well, *David*. But the Bible doesn't support that idea. It says "God shows no partiality."[36] He'll hear and save anybody who will put their trust in Him and His Word.

Can you imagine how different the lives of Absalom and Ahithophel could have been if, instead of avenging themselves, they'd looked to God as their defense? Great things could have happened! God could have moved on their behalf. Their relationship with David could have been restored. God could have exalted

[35] Psalm 55:17-19, 23
[36] Acts 10:34, NKJV

them to positions of honor and fulfilled His promises of blessing in their lives.

But unlike David, Absalom and Ahithophel didn't believe God's promises.

They didn't pay much attention to His warnings either.

God did warn them, you know...through a Bible story they'd undoubtedly heard many times: A story about another Israelite—a man named Korah—who once got upset with a God-anointed leader. Korah's chilling example should be enough to stop anybody from taking offense.

Back in the days after the exodus when the Israelites were tramping around the wilderness, Korah took offense at Moses for getting too uppity. It sounds silly, I realize; but from Korah's perspective Moses was treating his fellow Israelites like second class citizens: Moses issued commandments. He gave directions, and behaved in general like God had put him in charge.

Indignant, Korah polled his fellow Hebrews and found 250 who agreed with him. (You can always find people who will agree with you about an offense.) So together they set out to pull Moses off his high horse. They confronted him and said:

You have gone too far! Everyone in Israel has been set apart by the LORD, and he is with all of us. What right do you have to act as though you are greater than anyone else among all these people of the LORD?...Isn't it enough that you brought us out of Egypt, a land flowing with milk and honey, to kill us here in this wilderness, and that you now treat us like your subjects? (Numbers 16:3, 13).

Moses, of course, was horrified and hurt by the people's accusations. But he refused to strike back in his own defense. Instead he took the matter to the Lord.

Twenty-four hours later, Korah and Company found themselves on the wrong side of the no-weapon-formed-against-you-shall-prosper sword. In a dramatic scene designed to mark people's thinking forever:

> The ground suddenly split open beneath them...and swallowed the men, along with their households and the followers who were standing with them, and everything they owned. So they went down alive into the grave, along with their belongings. The earth closed over them, and they all vanished (vv. 31-33).

Absalom and Ahithophel would have been wise to give that ground-splitting incident some thought. I can almost guarantee you that David did. He was famous for meditating on God's Word. He believed its promises and heeded its warnings.

That's why, in the end, he triumphed. His enemies were defeated, he returned to Jerusalem, and reigned there as king for the rest of his life.

Too bad Absalom and Ahithophel didn't leave that kind of legacy. They should have taken a tip from Jude. When the devil invited them to return evil for evil and step onto the dark side, they should have said, "Never!"

We should too.

> Korah and Company found themselves on the wrong side of the no-weapon-formed-against-you-shall-prosper sword.

5

THE UNTOUCHABLES

For see, today I have made you immune to their attacks. You are strong like a fortified city that cannot be captured, like an iron pillar or a bronze wall. None...will be able to stand against you. They will try, but they will fail. For I am with you, and I will take care of you.
I, the LORD, have spoken!
Jeremiah 1:18-19

Think for a moment what it would be like to waltz through life immune to every kind of harm. Imagine how free and secure you would feel if you could live surrounded by a supernatural wall of protection that kept you absolutely safe from the garbage that comes at you in one way or another every single day.

Wouldn't that be awesome?

You wouldn't get irritated at people because they couldn't hurt you. You wouldn't have to defend yourself or lash out when somebody did you wrong because it would be unnecessary. Confident that all the enemy's plans against you are doomed to fail, you could stop fretting about them and concentrate on doing what God has called you to do. You could spend every day focused on fulfilling your purpose, secure in the knowledge that you are—in a much more vital way than Elliot Ness ever was—*untouchable*.

To many Christians, such a life sounds too good to be true. But it's not. It's the kind life that belongs to every believer. God said so in the Bible. Again and again, He made promises like these:

- No weapon turned against you will succeed (Isaiah 54:17).
- If you make the LORD your refuge, if you make the Most High your shelter, no evil will conquer you (Psalm 91:9-10).
- You will be blessed wherever you go, both in coming and in going. The LORD will conquer your enemies when they attack you. They will attack you from one direction, but they will

scatter from you in seven! (Deuteronomy 28. 6-7).
- He who has been born of God keeps himself, and the wicked one does not touch him (1 John 5:18 NKJV).
- And nothing shall by any means hurt you (Luke 10:19).

For years, I read such verses thinking they only promised protection from things like car accidents, terrorist attacks, or other physical dangers. But the fact is they cover every aspect of our being—spirit, soul, and body. They promise us protection from every kind of harm. That includes insults, irritations, rejections, betrayals, violations, offenses, and emotional attacks of all sorts.

According to the Bible, none of those things have the power to hurt us. They have no ability to thwart any part of God's plan for our lives. They can't capture us, conquer us, or injure us in any way.

Unless we let them, that is.

Which most of us must admit we often do.

"Well, I can't help it," you might say. "Some people just get to me. They do and say things that drive me nuts!"

No, they can't drive you nuts unless you choose to allow it. They can't get to you unless you make yourself vulnerable by reacting in a way that blasts a hole in your wall of divine protection. As long as you keep your eyes on the promises of God and walk in obedience to

His Word, you can live like you're coated with spiritual Teflon. Nothing anybody else does can stick to you. You can walk through life as a living demonstration of the Psalm 119:165: "Great peace have they which love thy law: and nothing shall offend them."[37]

In other words, you can live like Jesus did when He was on earth.

Talk about being immune to attacks! Jesus was the ultimate Untouchable when it came to dealing with the ugly stuff other people said and did. Take, for example, how He responded to the way the people in His hometown of Nazareth treated Him. They got so mad at Him when He preached in the synagogue that they decided to put a permanent end to His ministry.

> Jumping up, they mobbed him and took him to the edge of the hill on which the city was built. They intended to push him over the cliff, but he slipped away through the crowd and left them...He walked right through [them] and went on his way (Luke 4:29-30, NLT, NIV).

Think of it! An entire mob of people tried to murder Jesus that day. But not one of them could lay a hand on Him. They couldn't touch His body and they couldn't harm His soul because He put His trust in God. He stayed continually in the Secret Place of the Most High.

If we're ever tempted to doubt that God meant what He said in His promises of protection, all we

---

[37] KJV

have to do is look at Jesus. He lived His entire life like a fortified city that cannot be captured. Mistreatment bounced off Him like He was an iron pillar or a bronze wall. Nobody could ever stand against Him. He enjoyed such unfailing victory that He had to choose to lay down His life for the devil to get at Him. And even then He could say, "The devil has nothing in Me. He has no power over me."³⁸

JESUS DIDN'T HAVE AN EDGE ON US

"But Vikki, that was Jesus! We can't live like He did!"

He said we can.

Before He went to the cross He told His disciples, "Anyone who believes in me will do the same works I have done, and even greater works, because I am going to be with the Father."³⁹ He wasn't just talking about working miracles when He said that, either. He was telling us we can live His lifestyle.

> We think Jesus had an edge on us. We assume He had special advantages because of His deity. But that's not true.

And if He said we could do it, then it's possible.

We sometimes find that hard to believe because we think Jesus had an edge on us. We assume He had special advantages because of His deity. But that's not

---
³⁸ John 14:30, NKJ, NLT
³⁹ John 14:12

true. Jesus came to earth as a man. He laid down His divine privileges and took on the limits of humanity. (See Philippians 2:6-7.) He humbled Himself and lived like a human being so that He could show us how to live victoriously on the earth.

His life was no bed of roses, either. He faced more trouble than we ever will. The Bible says He was a man of sorrows and acquainted with grief.[40] (That doesn't mean He saw grief from afar; it means He experienced it!) The leaders of His day came against Him. His family persecuted Him. He endured so much pressure in the Garden of Gethsemane that blood came out of His pores.

You and I have never experienced that much pressure and we never will. So, really, we have it easier than Jesus did. We have His Blood to make us righteous. We have the Word of God to instruct us. We have the Holy Spirit living in us and the gifts of the Spirit to help us. We have every advantage our Savior had and a less strenuous assignment to fulfill. No wonder the Scripture says we're more than conquerors through Him!

"Yes, but Jesus had a lot more revelation than we do. He knew what to do in every situation because He was God's Son!"

Who do you think you are? Aren't you a son of God too? Doesn't the Bible say that you have the mind of Christ?[41]

---

[40] Isaiah 53:3
[41] 1 Corinthians 2:16

Sure it does. You just need to develop that mind by spending time in the Scriptures and in fellowship with God.

That's what Jesus did. Wisdom didn't come instantly to Him any more than it does to you and me. He had to grow in it.[42] He had to study the Word of God. He had to practice walking by faith in that Word and following the leading of the Spirit moment by moment the same way we do.

Jesus wasn't born with a divine Daytimer all filled out with goals, plans, and instructions. He didn't walk around knowing everything that was about to happen. The night of the storm, for instance, when He got into the boat with the disciples and said, "Let's cross to the other side of the lake."[43] He probably figured like we usually do that it was going to be an uneventful night.

God hadn't laid out the entire agenda for Him and said, "Okay, first you're going to get in the boat. You'll sail for a while and then hit some wild weather. When that happens, you'll say to the winds and waves, 'Peace, be still.' Then you'll get to the other side of the sea and meet a demon possessed man. And there will be some pigs there..."

No. God doesn't give us that much information all at once and He didn't give it to Jesus either. He had to walk out His life the same way we do, one step at a time. Most likely, Jesus only had one simple leading when He got into the boat on the Sea of Galilee that

---
[42] "And Jesus increased in wisdom and stature, and in favour with God and man." Luke 2:52, KJV
[43] Luke 4:35

night: *Go to the other side*. He knew that meant God had a divine assignment for Him there so when the storm came up, He didn't panic. He just dealt with the problem by faith. He had sense enough to know that God wasn't going to send Him on a mission and then drown Him in the middle of the lake.

I wish more Christians had that much sense!

> We need to realize we actually are on a mission from God. That's something Jesus knew and never forgot for a single moment.

If we did, we'd stop letting the so-called crises of life upset us. We'd say, "Oh yeah, this is like the storm that tried to stop Jesus. So I'll just do what He did. I'll speak to it and make it calm down."

To face life's storms with that kind of boldness, however, we need to realize we actually are on a mission from God. That's something Jesus knew and never forgot for a single moment. It was one of the primary secrets to His success. He understood that "For this purpose the Son of God was manifested, that he might destroy the works of the devil."[44] And nothing could divert Him from that purpose. It was His destiny and His destination in life. No matter how many roadblocks the devil threw in His way, no matter how many physical or emotional storms He encountered, He refused to take a detour.

---

[44] 1 John 3:8, KJV

DON'T DRIVE AROUND UNTIL YOU RUN OUT OF GAS

This is not only true about Jesus, it's true about everybody: People of purpose are not easily detoured. When we know where we're headed we can stay on the right road.

It's just logical. If you're driving from Dallas and you've identified your destination as Los Angeles, you're not going to follow signs that direct you to New York. Those signs will take you the wrong way. How do you know? Because you're clear about where you're going.

The same thing is true in life. But here's the problem: Most people haven't identified their destination. So they end up driving all over the place trying to figure out what roads they should take. Eventually they just run out of gas.

Jesus didn't make that mistake. He found out exactly what He was called to do. He spent time in prayer and the Word getting God's agenda for His life. He sought His Father's guidance every single day about what He should do and say. Sometimes He prayed all night to find out those things.

Once He knew, He didn't do anything else. He didn't let other people drag Him into their activities, arguments, or upsets. He never let anyone agitate Him, offend Him, or distract Him from His mission.

They tried, though. Oh, how they tried! The Pharisees and Sadducees badgered Him without mercy. They criticized Him and plotted against Him. They baited Him with theological questions: What do you think about divorce? What do you think about paying taxes? What's the most important commandment?

But Jesus never got sucked into their schemes. He never fell into their traps. Because He only cared about fulfilling His purpose and pleasing God, His critics couldn't take Him captive with their opinions and accusations. "Your approval or disapproval means nothing to me," He told them.[45] Then He went on carrying out His Father's business, completely free.

If we adopt the same attitude, we can walk in the same freedom and victory He did. We can say yes to the will of God and no to everything else. We can stay on course and fulfill our destiny, regardless of what anybody else does or thinks.

> "Your approval or disapproval means nothing to me," He told them. Then He went on carrying out His Father's business, completely free.

Truth be told, pleasing people is impossible anyway. Every one of them has a different idea about what we should be doing—and those ideas change about every five minutes. So we can run ourselves ragged trying to make them happy today only to find out they want something else tomorrow.

Proverbs 29:25 says, "The fear of man brings a snare." But we can steer clear of that snare the way

---

[45] John 5:41

the Master did: By refusing to worry about what other people think of us. In the eternal scheme of things their opinion doesn't matter. God's opinion is the only one that counts. He's the One who blesses us. He's the One who provides for us. He's the One we will ultimately answer to. So if He's pleased with us why should it matter what the Pharisees and Sadducees in our life are saying?

Although I don't tell people this to their face, when somebody's trying to distract or discourage me from my God-ordained mission I often say it on the inside: "I don't care what you think about me. You're not going to be there with me when I stand before God someday. You won't be there when I have to explain that I didn't do what He told me because you didn't like it. So you can criticize me if you want but I'm going to focus on His approval not yours."

I'll never forget the first time I found out how freeing that mindset can be. I'd just started a new season of my life when, after homeschooling my daughter through her elementary school and junior high years, I'd enrolled her in a Christian school. Suddenly, I had extra hours available to me. And because God had already given me direction, I knew what He wanted me to do with them.

But then an unexpected opportunity arose.

A woman at our church invited me to be a part of a new and exciting committee. The committee was being formed to provide input to the Mayor of Fort Worth about policy decisions. Made up of people from various walks of life, the group would be meeting regularly with the Mayor to offer their perspective. I was asked to represent the homeschooling community.

It was an attractive and flattering invitation. Hobnobbing with the Mayor struck me as a very prestigious thing to do. And I did know a lot about homeschooling. I'd done it for a long time and my daughter had a 4.0 average as she entered her new school so, apparently, I'd done a good job. There were a lot of reasons for me to jump at the opportunity.

But one thing stopped me: My mission. I knew where I was headed and all I could think was, *This has absolutely nothing to do with God's call on my life.*

So I said no. I did my best to be gracious about it. "I'm so honored that out of all the homeschooling parents you know you would ask me to sit on this committee," I said. "But it's not my place. It doesn't line up with where I'm headed and what I'm doing in life. If I took that position, I'd be denying the right person of it." Then I prayed with the woman and we asked God to help her find the person He had in mind.

She's a wonderful lady so she didn't get upset with me or try to argue with me about my decision. But even if she had, I wouldn't have changed my mind. I would have declined the offer and stayed on the right road for one simple reason: because I knew my destination.

NOT INSANE...JUST IMMUNE

If you don't know your God-given purpose yet, then seek God about it with everything that's in you. Make it your quest in life to discover your divine purpose. Pray, spend time in God's Word, and fellowship with Him until you identify His direction for your life.

I'll warn you in advance: that may take some time. It certainly did for me. After I burned myself out living like a workaholic, doing a thousand things God never told me to do and living to please everybody but Him, it took me some time to find God's plan. He wasn't hiding it from me; I just couldn't hear what He was saying for a while. My mind was too full of static. The list of *Things to Do* that continually ricocheted around in my brain kept drowning out His voice.

But I stuck with my quest and soon found my God-ordained mission.

Maybe you've been wandering around for so long without a definite sense of purpose you're not confident anymore that God even has a mission for you. But I guarantee you He does. He has assignments for us all and every one of them is significant. They may not all rank high on the world's scale of "greatness," but so what? That scale is bogus anyway. It's just manmade hogwash. The reality is that anything

God tells you to do is important—not because of what it is but because of Who told you to do it.

Once you find your divine purpose everything else will drop away. Your path will start becoming clear. You may not know everything about it. In fact, I promise you, you won't. But with a general understanding of where you're going, the path will become visible one step at a time.

If, on the other hand, you just keep driving through life without a destination, doing what everybody else says you should do or reacting to the offenses that come at you, you're sure to go the wrong way and miss out on your destiny. You'll end up like the children of Israel that Moses led out of Egypt. They turned an eleven day journey to the Promised Land into a 40 year trip and still failed to reach their destination.

Wouldn't it be tragic to wake up one morning and realize you'd wasted 40 years?

Yes, it would.

I can testify to it because I did something like that myself. I wasted years in ministry thinking I was serving God when I was really just fulfilling my own self-appointed agenda. I felt the loss of knowing those years were gone and I couldn't get them back. (You can read more about this in my book *Some Days You Dance*.)

It's a sobering thought, isn't it? One we may not like to consider. But whether we like to think about it or not, the Bible makes this clear: Whatever we build with our lives will ultimately be measured—not against our own ideas or other people's opinions and judgments but against the plans God had for us.

> If anyone builds...with gold, silver, precious stones, wood, hay, straw, each one's work will become clear; for the Day will declare it, because it will be revealed by fire; and the fire will test each one's work, of what sort it is. If anyone's work which he has built on it endures, he will receive a reward. If anyone's work is burned, he will suffer loss; but he himself will be saved, yet so as through fire...Therefore we make it our aim, whether present or absent, to be well pleasing to Him. For we must all appear before the judgment seat of Christ, that each one may receive the things done in the body, according to what he has done, whether good or bad (1 Corinthians 3:13-15, 2 Corinthians 5:9-10).

If we want to receive lots of eternal rewards, we'll build according to the blueprint Jesus gave us. He sought God and found out where He was headed. He discovered His purpose and then refused to allow anybody else's words or actions distract Him from it.

I said it before and I'll say it again: People of purpose aren't easily detoured. They aren't easily offended. They don't wear their feelings on their shoulder and they don't have time to mess with folks who want to fuss and fight. They're too focused on the Word of God and too busy fulfilling their mission.

That's how Jesus was and it's how we can be too. We can become such people of purpose that if somebody insults us, we don't even notice. If it dawns on us later what happened, we'll just laugh. "You mean that person meant to hurt my feelings and I didn't even get it?" we'll say. "How funny is that?!"

Then we'll turn our attention right back to our divine assignment. We'll waltz on through life as if nothing bad could ever touch us.

People who see us laughing in the face of insults and offenses may accuse us of being just a little bit insane. But that's okay. We know better. We're not suffering from insanity. We're just enjoying the immunity God promised.

We're like a fortified city that can't be captured.

Like Jesus...we are free.

6

IT'S NOTHING PERSONAL

A final word: Be strong with the Lord's mighty power. Put on all of God's armor so that you will be able to stand firm against all strategies and tricks of the Devil. For we are not fighting against people made of flesh and blood, but against the evil rulers and authorities of the unseen world, against those mighty powers of darkness who rule this world, and against wicked spirits in the heavenly realms.
Ephesians 6:10-12

I have nothing against Donald Trump. In fact, for a while I was a big fan of his television show. So I'd never suggest there's any kind of connection between Donald and the devil. But sometimes when watching *The Apprentice* it has occurred to me that the two of them do have one particular trait in common.

Mr. Trump drops the hammer on aspiring entrepreneurs with the same indifference that marks the devil's attacks on believers. Only one of them uses the words "You're fired!" But either might be likely to add the other phrase that Mr. Trump has coined:

"It's nothing personal. It's just business."

Having never appeared on *The Apprentice*, I don't know firsthand what it's like to be booted off of the show. But I've noticed this about those who do. Regardless of what Mr. Trump says, they seem to take it very personally.

The same is often true for believers. When the devil attacks us, we tend to feel it in an extremely personal way. Instead of evaluating the situation from a spiritual perspective in the light of what the Bible says, we let our flesh take over. We pin the blame on whoever the devil used to hurt us. Then we get mad at them.

If we want to live in victory like Jesus did, however, we have to be smarter than that. We have to remember we're in the midst of a conflict between the Kingdom of Darkness and the Kingdom of Light. And the mistreatment we experience originates—always and only—with Satan himself.

> For we are not fighting against people made of flesh and blood, but against the evil rulers and authorities of the unseen world, against those mighty powers of darkness who rule this world, and against wicked spirits in the heavenly realms (Ephesians 6:12).

This is what kept Jesus cool and composed in the face of criticism, accusations, betrayals, and threats: He knew they were nothing personal. They were just evidence that the prince of darkness is still doing business the same old way. He's still trying to ambush God's people with offense and divert them from their destiny. He's still telling this old, familiar lie: *You'd better start looking out for Number One or you're not going to make it. You'd better forget what God said and fight for yourself or you're going to end up suffering some serious permanent harm.*

Do you know who first heard that lie?

Eve.

And, amazingly enough, she believed it.

Most of us still wonder why on earth she did. At the time, she didn't have any real reason to be concerned about her well-being. She and Adam were living the high life in the Garden of Eden. They had full access to the riches of God. They had a perfect marriage and lived in the world's most exquisite resort. They didn't even have to cook; the food grew on trees.

Even so, when the devil showed up in the form of a serpent and started chatting with Eve, she was taken in by his deception.

"Really?" he asked [her]. "Did God really say you must not eat any of the fruit in the garden?"

"Of course we may eat it," [she] told him. "It's only the fruit from the tree at the center of the garden that we are not allowed to eat. God says we must not eat it or even touch it, or we will die."

"You won't die!" the serpent hissed. "God knows that your eyes will be opened when you eat it. You will become just like God, knowing everything, both good and evil" (Genesis 3:1-5).

That conversation is so familiar to most of us that we sometimes neglect to consider all the implications of it. But think for a moment: How would you feel if you found out that someone you trusted completely had lied to you? What emotions would you experience if you discovered they'd taken advantage of you, played you for a fool, and deprived you of a priceless blessing?

You'd be shocked, wouldn't you? You'd feel hurt, violated, and betrayed. And that's exactly the reaction the devil was hoping to produce in Eve. He wanted her to get offended with God. It's not that the devil had anything against her as an individual. Even back then his attacks weren't personal. It was just business. Satan wanted to rule the earth and the only way he could do it was to steal Adam and Eve's God-given dominion by deceiving them into switching kingdoms.

That's why he suggested to Eve that God's Word didn't really mean what she thought it meant. He introduced the question, "Did God really say?" because—as all of us who've ever entertained that question have discovered—it's deadly. Like a spiritual poison, it kills our faith in God's Word.

Eve could have chosen to reject that question. She could have done what we should all do when the devil tries to deceive us: Reminded herself of exactly what God had said, exercised her authority, and put the devil on the run.

She knew that's what she and Adam were supposed to do. God had specifically instructed them to "keep" the garden, which in Hebrew means *to guard, protect and keep it safe*. But Eve didn't do that. (Neither did her husband, who was standing right beside her the whole time.)

Instead of rebuking the serpent and kicking him out of Eden, Eve listened to him. She began to wonder, *What if God really didn't say what I thought He said? What if He didn't really mean that if I ate the fruit I would die?*

Don't ever fool around with such dangerous thoughts. The minute you catch yourself wondering about what God has said, grab your Bible and find out. Build yourself up on His promises. Remind yourself of His instructions. Put an end to the devil's questions before they put an end to your faith.

Although Eve didn't have a Bible to read, she had everything she needed to rid her mind of any doubts about God. She'd walked and talked with Him. She'd experienced His faithfulness and love. She'd been the beneficiary of His blessings every day of her life so she knew the spiritual truth. But she let the devil distract her from that truth with sensory information from the natural realm.

The Bible doesn't specifically say this, but I believe the devil did more than just talk to Eve. I think he touched the forbidden fruit to show her how harmless it was. He put it in front of her eyes so she could admire its beauty. He "proved" to her that she wouldn't die from touching it and that eating it would be to her advantage.

Sadly, his plan worked.

> The woman was convinced. The fruit looked so fresh and delicious, and it would make her so wise! So she ate some of the fruit. She also gave some to her husband, who was with her. Then he ate it, too. At that moment, their eyes were opened, and they suddenly felt shame at their nakedness. So they strung fig leaves together around their hips to cover themselves (vv. 6-7).

Just to set the record straight, Adam and Eve hadn't been strolling around the Garden naked and too naive to know it. Sin didn't wake them up to their nudity. Sin caused it! Before they disobeyed God they'd been clothed from the inside out with the light of His glory. But once they died spiritually, they experienced a wardrobe malfunction of epic proportions. The light that had covered them went out and they started grabbing fig leaves.

No doubt, you've heard of going from rags to riches. Adam and Eve did the reverse. They went from riches to rags in an instant—all because they switched kingdoms. They transferred themselves, through their disobedience, into the Kingdom of Darkness and out of the Kingdom of Light.

WHICH KINGDOM WILL YOU CHOOSE?

Imagine what would happen if you closed your account at the bank and transferred all your money somewhere else. You couldn't write checks on the old account or make withdrawals from your bank anymore, could you? If you tried, you'd be denied. The bank would refuse to give you any more money. Because you'd transferred your account, you would no longer have access to their resources.

Now imagine you quit your current job and went to work for another company. Then a few months later you went back to your previous employer asking to be paid. What response would you receive?

"Sorry, we don't owe you anything. You don't work here anymore."

In a nutshell that is what happened with Adam and Eve. They lost their access to God's presence, power, and provision because they transferred out of His system and into Satan's system. They switched kingdoms and exchanged the blessing for the curse.

Because we've all "sinned and come short of the glory of God,"[46] you and I would be in the same mess if it wasn't for this: Through Jesus, God made the way for us to get back into His kingdom. "For He delivered us from the domain of darkness, and transferred us to the kingdom of His beloved Son, in whom we have redemption, the forgiveness of sins."[47]

Why, then, does it seem like so many Christians are still living under the devil's thumb? Why aren't we enjoying all the blessing, protection, and victory that belong to us as joint heirs with Jesus in the kingdom of God?

> Why aren't we enjoying all the blessing, protection, and victory that belong to us as joint heirs with Jesus in the kingdom of God?

Because much of the time we're still acting and thinking according to the devil's lies. We're still operating in his system and voluntarily giving him dominion over us. As Romans 6:16 says, "When you offer yourselves to someone to obey him as slaves, you are slaves to the one whom you obey—whether you are slaves to sin, which leads to death, or to obedience, which leads to righteousness."[48]

We need to stay out of the devil's system! We need to stop letting him drag us back into his way of doing

---

[46] Romans 3:23, KJV
[47] Colossians 1:13-14, NASB
[48] NIV

things, wise up to his tricks, and live like children of Light!

That means we can't just read and forget what the Bible says about the spiritual battle we're in. We can't just go on with our lives without paying any attention to the kingdom conflict going on around us. If we do, six months from now we'll look around to find that we've fallen back into the devil's traps. We'll realize we've gotten crossways with somebody who's done us wrong and once again been rendered useless to the Kingdom of God.

To live in victory we must continually be aware of the enemy we're fighting. We must remember all the time that it's kingdom against kingdom, and decide every day which side we're going to be on. When we get up in the morning, we should say, "I'm living in God's Kingdom today. I'm operating according to His principles. I refuse to give the devil any place in me."

That's the way Jesus lived. He stayed continuously alert to the fact that He was in a spiritual fight. He always remembered when He encountered offensive situations that Satan was the root of them; people were just the fruit. So He looked beyond the people to the author of the attacks. He waged his warfare directly against the Kingdom of Darkness.

Think about how He responded when John the Baptist was murdered, for instance. Jesus had every reason to take that attack personally. John was His cousin! He was a loved one and a co-laborer in ministry. Yet Jesus didn't lash out in any way at the people responsible for John's death. He didn't grab a sword and slaughter Herod like Herod had slaughtered John. Jesus didn't even preach any Herod-bashing sermons.

It's amazing, really. Jesus felt the same emotions we do. How angry would it make you to find out someone dear to you had been killed in such a horrific way? How heartbroken would you be if one of your loved ones had their head chopped off and delivered to a demonic woman on a silver platter?

Jesus must have hurt to the core!

But you know what He did?

> As soon as Jesus heard the news, he went off by himself in a boat to a remote area to be alone. But the crowds heard where he was headed and followed by land from many villages. A vast crowd was there as he stepped from the boat, and he had compassion on them and healed their sick (Matthew 14:13-14).

Even though His heart was aching, Jesus refused to respond according to the devil's system. He refused to get angry at the people who wronged Him and be drawn into the trap of offense. Instead He chose to retaliate in a different way. He struck back, not against flesh and blood but against his real enemy. By praying for people, loving them, and healing them, He destroyed the works of the devil and won a victory for the Kingdom of Light.

Think about that next time you're hurt, wounded, and cut to the core. Respond like Jesus did. Go after the root and not the fruit. Say, "Devil, you'll be sorry you ever heard my name. You'll wish you'd never come near me because now I'm on a mission to steal more people than ever out of your kingdom."

Then do whatever the Holy Spirit leads you to do. Go to the mall and start witnessing to people. Hit the beach or the street and tell everybody in sight about the goodness of God. Choose to retaliate in the spirit instead of reacting in the flesh.

That's the choice Jesus always made. No matter how personal the attacks may have felt, He never got into the wrong kingdom. He never took offense and started beating up people. He stayed in the secret place of the Most High, inaccessible to the Kingdom of Darkness.

He remembered He was in a spiritual fight and made the devil pay.

DON'T HANG YOURSELF THIS THANKSGIVING

One thing that kept Jesus from getting mad at the people who caused Him trouble was this: He realized they didn't know what was going on. They were ignorant of the kingdom conflict and had no idea they were being used by the devil. (That's why on the cross, Jesus could pray, "Father, forgive these people, because they don't know what they are doing."[49])

Even the Pharisees who harassed Jesus didn't consciously set out to serve the Kingdom of Darkness. They were operating strictly in the flesh. They were just jealous of Him and afraid He was going to ruin the religious

---
[49] Luke 23:24

con game they'd been running. When they tried to trap Him by grilling Him with hostile questions,[50] they didn't realize there was a kingdom behind those questions. The same can be said about the people who act ugly toward you. They don't know who's inciting them to do it. When they mistreat you or accuse you, it never occurs to them they're being goaded into it by The Accuser[51] himself.

> Even the Pharisees who harassed Jesus didn't consciously set out to serve the Kingdom of Darkness. They were operating strictly in the flesh.

You do, though. And you can never afford to let yourself forget it.

Especially around the holidays.

In my experience that's often when the devil lays some of his sneakiest traps. He usually does it through unsaved (or just plain ornery) relatives.

You might be enjoying a perfectly nice Thanksgiving meal when one of them looks across the table at you and says, "If you were really a Christian…" The next thing you know you're being baited. Your relatives are dangling a verbal noose in front of you. (In Greek, the word *accuse* can literally refer to putting a noose around the neck.) You try for a moment to hold your tongue. Then your blood starts to boil and suddenly

---

[50] Luke 11:53-54
[51] Rev. 12:10

you're in an argument with a room full of spiritual ignoramuses. You're hanging yourself with your own angry words while somewhere the devil is smiling and saying, "Gotcha!"

I don't mean this unkindly at all, but arguing with unspiritual people about spiritual things is pointless. They don't know what they're talking about. That realization hit me years ago when my unsaved brother called me a hypocrite.

"Do you even know what a hypocrite is?" I replied.

He admitted he couldn't really define it.

"Fine," I said, "you don't even know what you're calling me. What if a hypocrite was a good thing?"

He didn't want to risk calling me something good so that's where the conversation ended.

Here's a word to the wise: If you have trouble keeping your cool in such situations, stay out of them. You don't have to be rude about it. You don't have to ignore your cantankerous relatives completely. Just maintain a safe emotional distance, and when you're with them steer clear of potentially hot topics of discussion.

> Here's a word to the wise: If you have trouble keeping your cool in such situations, stay out of them.

"If I do that," you might ask, "how can I convince them to believe on Jesus? How can I persuade them turn their lives around?"

You can't...and that's okay because it's not your responsibility.

"But I love my relatives! I want them to get saved!"

I understand. I feel the same way about mine. But I never experienced real freedom until I realized I'm not responsible for what they do with their lives. They're accountable for their own choices. My responsibility is to pray for them and follow after God.

Once I recognized that, the devil couldn't use my family to trap me anymore. I could leave them free to think, say, and do whatever they pleased without letting it have a negative effect on me.

Of course, if God told me to call them on the phone and say something specific to them I would. But He's rarely led me to do it. I eventually figured out why. Jesus said, "A prophet has no honor in his own country,"[52] and believers rarely get any respect from their relatives. The unsaved ones, in particular, loathe listening to us. Because we're their sister, child, cousin, aunt, (or whatever), they don't want us telling them what to do or how to think.

So most of the time the wisest course of action is just to pray for them. That's what I've done for my family over the years. Instead arguing with them, I pray earnestly that the Holy Spirit would move them toward Jesus. I say, "Visit them in the night, Lord! Give them spiritual dreams. Flood their room with Your love right this minute so they can't deny Your

---

[52] John 4:44, NKJV

existence. Bring laborers to them who will share the Gospel with them in a way that they can receive it."

If God sends me to be one of those laborers, I'm happy to share the Word with them. But, as I said, He usually doesn't, because my unsaved family members don't want to hear it from me. Odds are, yours don't want to hear it from you, either.

If you want to bless them, just focus on your own personal growth in the Lord. Concentrate on fulfilling your destiny. As you spend your time learning to live the way God has called you to live, you'll be changed. Then, next Thanksgiving when your relatives look at you across the table they'll see the peace of God on your face. They'll see His love and His joy in your eyes. Your life will become a testimony they cannot deny.

That's what happened to me with my brother. He'd disliked me almost all my life. Actually, because I grew up in an abusive home, all my siblings were at odds with each other. When we were kids, my brother chased me down the street with a butcher's knife in his hand. He meant business with it, too. I dodge into my friend's house, run into the bathroom, and slam the door to get away from him. Then I heard the knife hit the door and think, *Whew! Saved again!*

Then when I gave my life to the Lord, his dislike for me skyrocketed. I was no fun anymore. Every time he was near me conviction overwhelmed him. The light of God in me showed up the darkness in him and made him miserable. At family gatherings when I'd sit down next to him and he'd get up and walk away.

Romans 12:18 says "Do your part to live in peace with everyone, as much as possible." In my relationship with my brother I did my part. But he didn't make it easy.

Shortly after I gave my life to the Lord, I called to let him know that Dennis and I were moving from California to Texas. "I just wanted to tell you I love you," I said.

"Well, I hate you!" he replied.

> I called to let him know that Dennis and I were moving from California to Texas. "I just wanted to tell you I love you," I said. "Well, I hate you!" he replied.

For ten years he didn't speak to me. Then one day seemingly out of the blue he called me on the phone. When I answered he didn't even bother to say hello. He just blurted out these words: "You want to know why I hate you?"

"Yes, I do," I said. "I've been wondering that for a long time."

"I hate you because you have so much peace in your life."

Of course! I thought. My brother had never had that kind of peace. He was alcoholic. The day he called me he'd just spent time in lock-up after being arrested by the police department for threatening to kill himself. I'm sure he wanted to experience for himself the peace he sensed when he was around me but he'd always been too proud to ask me about it.

Once he opened the door, though, I leapt through it. "You can have the same peace I do," I said. "It's available to you and anybody else who will take it."

That was an awesome moment. But I would have forfeited it if I hadn't worked so hard to live at peace with him. If I'd taken his insults personally, put my neck in the noose, and hung myself by saying something he could use against me, he wouldn't have called me that day. I might never have gotten the opportunity to share the Gospel with him.

Maybe no such opportunities have come your way yet. Maybe your relatives are still grilling you with hostile questions and looking for ways to hurt you. If so, be patient. Cut them some slack. They don't really know what's going on. They have no idea they're caught in the middle of a kingdom conflict.

But you do. You not only know you're in a spiritual fight, you know that every victory will bring eternal rewards.

So set your heart on winning. When the attacks come, remember it's not personal; they're the work of the devil and for him this is just business. Then respond to his attacks by exacting some revenge in the realm of the spirit. Love on somebody. Pray for somebody. Tell somebody who's hurting about the goodness of the Lord.

Live like a child of the Light and show the Kingdom of Darkness that you mean business too.

7

DON'T LET THE DEVIL DEFUSE YOUR DREAM

Jesus turned to Peter and said, "Get away from me, Satan! You are a dangerous trap to me. You are seeing things merely from a human point of view, and not from God's."
Matthew 16:23 Phillips

One day when a friend of mine was praying fervently for her troubled teenage son, she asked God a question. "Why is the devil so determined to destroy him, Lord?"

Considering the circumstances, it's easy to see why she asked. Almost everybody in the boy's life—teachers, church leaders, and friends—had suddenly turned against him. Dealing him one emotional blow after another, they'd left him feeling dazed and abandoned, even by God.

At school, authorities had accused him of a theft he didn't commit. At church, a youth pastor had heard about the accusations and banished him from the youth group. His peers believed the rumors and turned their backs on him too.

My friend knew it was a strategy of the devil. But she couldn't figure out the reason for it. Why would one, normal, God-loving, church-going, 17 year-old boy merit such attacks? Asking her heavenly Father for an explanation, she waited to hear His voice.

The answer He gave her is one we would all do well to remember.

"Your son carries within him the power to do great damage to the Kingdom of Darkness," He said. "That power is ticking like a time bomb on the inside of him. The devil is desperate to defuse it before it goes off."

Those same words could be said about you, me, and every other child of God.

Each one of us is a constant threat to the devil's dominion. We may look on the outside like just a bunch of average Joes. But on the inside, because we carry God's Word and the anointing of the Holy Spirit, we're more like an army of *Josephs*. And Satan knows from experience how much trouble they can be.

The first Joseph he encountered (the one in the Old Testament) carried a time bomb of God's Word inside him too. It had been planted in his heart as a teenager in the form of a dream, and contained enough divine power to guide the boy's life, save his family, and deliver a nation.

From the beginning, the devil worked frantically to defuse it. Employing his old, familiar tactics, he made sure that Joseph was mistreated. He blindsided him with betrayals and laid sinister traps of offense. But Joseph didn't fall prey to them. Instead he staked out a path of success we can all follow. He ended up living a dream come true.

Not that Joseph was perfect. He wasn't. In fact, as a teenager he made some seriously dumb mistakes. He not only opened the door for the devil, he practically set out a *Welcome* mat, by opening his big mouth and sharing his God-given dream...at the wrong time...with the wrong people. Less than 24 hours after he had his first God-given dream, Joseph promptly reported it, in detail, to his brothers.

I don't know why he did it.

Maybe he was just naïve. Maybe he suffered from a touch of youthful arrogance. Maybe the favoritism his father showed him had affected his judgment. Whatever the reason, Joseph ignored the fact that his brothers already hated him and announced to them without a shred of wisdom, "Listen to this dream I had! We were out in the field tying up bundles of grain. My bundle stood up, and then your bundles all gathered around and bowed low before it!"

His brothers' response was painful but predictable, "'So you are going to be our king, are you?' they taunted. And they hated him all the more for his dream and what he had said."[53]

If you want to avoid unnecessary agitation in life, you might want to make a mental note to yourself: Don't share your God-given dreams with people who won't appreciate them. Instead, keep quiet, nurture those dreams in prayer, and strengthen them with the Word. It will save you a lot of grief.

Obviously, young Joseph didn't yet have such a note in his mental files. What's worse, he was a slow learner. Even after his jeering brothers dialed up their hatred of him a few notches, he did the same thing again. Having received yet another nocturnal word from God, he ran to them with a report. "'Listen to this dream,' he said. 'The sun, moon, and eleven stars bowed low before me!'"[54]

This time, Joseph's brothers decided they'd had all they could stand. Fed up with his dreams of grandeur, they conspired to get rid of him. "Come on, let's kill him and throw him into a deep pit," they said. "We can tell our father that a wild animal has eaten him. Then we'll see what becomes of all his dreams!"[55]

When it comes to dysfunctional families, this bunch takes the prize.

---

[53] Genesis 37:6-8
[54] vv. 9-10
[55] vv. 19, 20

The only reason Joseph survived was because they eventually decided it made more sense to sell him than to kill him. So they made a deal with some wandering Ishmaelites who were in the market for a slave, and went home happy—free of their boastful little brother, and a few bucks richer to boot.

The devil probably brushed his hands together as he watched the Ishmaelites carry Joseph away in chains and thought, *There! That should put an end to his dreams!*

> The only reason Joseph survived was because they eventually decided it made more sense to sell him than to kill him.

He would have been right, too, if Joseph had responded like believers often do. If he had spent the rest of his life hurt and angry about his brothers' betrayal, he would have lost sight of God's promise of promotion. He would have withered away in bitterness as a forgotten slave in a foreign land.

But that's not what happened.

Forced to choose between his feelings and his God-ordained future, Joseph focused on his future. He kept his dream alive. He continued to believe in his destiny even when everyone around him doubted. Refusing to let the cruelty and injustice he'd suffered affect his heart, he decided that instead of playing the part of a victim—which he had every right to do—he would chose another role.

He would fulfill God's plan and become a deliverer instead.

Few of us have ever suffered the kinds of abuses Joseph did. Our relatives might have hurt us, but most of us don't have leaves of murder and human trafficking hanging from our family tree. So Joseph's example can inspire us. Surely if he found a way to escape the trap of offense and keep his eyes on his dream, we can too.

A REAL-LIFE DESPERATE HOUSEWIFE

The Bible says, "The eyes of the Lord search back and forth across the whole earth, looking for people whose hearts are perfect toward him, so that he can show his great power in helping them."[56] In the original Hebrew text, the word *perfect* doesn't refer to performance. It means *committed*. Surprisingly enough, it also means *peaceful and quiet*.

That's the kind of heart Joseph had. He was so committed to his God and his dream that he let peace rule inside even when trouble broke loose on the outside. He maintained his quiet trust in God even when he had every reason to boil with resentment.

As a result, God showed Himself strong on Joseph's behalf. When the Ishmaelites sold him to Potiphar, a member of the personal staff of Pharaoh and captain of the palace guard:

> The LORD was with Joseph and blessed him greatly as he served in the home of his

---
[56] 2 Chronicles 16:9, TLB

Egyptian master. Potiphar noticed this and realized that the LORD was with Joseph, giving him success in everything he did. So Joseph naturally became quite a favorite with him. Potiphar soon put Joseph in charge of his entire household and entrusted him with all his business dealings. From the day Joseph was put in charge, the LORD began to bless Potiphar for Joseph's sake (Genesis 39:2-5).

This should be the story of every Christian employee. Bosses everywhere should be purposely hiring believers because they bring God's blessing on their businesses. CEOs all over the world should be pointing to the Christians in their offices and saying, "They're my favorites. Everything they touch becomes a success!"

> A real-life desperate housewife, she eyed Joseph's handsome face and well-built body, and lusted after him.

Potiphar certainly said it. He loved Joseph!

There was just one problem. Mrs. Potiphar did too. A real-life desperate housewife, she eyed Joseph's handsome face and well-built body, and lusted after him. (I didn't make that up. It's in the Bible.) She pressured him day after day to sleep with her.

Unwilling to sin against God and against Potiphar in such a shocking way, Joseph refused.

He kept out of her way as much as possible. One day, however, no one else was around when he was doing his work inside the house. She came and grabbed him by his shirt, demanding, "Sleep with me!" Joseph tore himself away, but as he did, his shirt came off. She was left holding it as he ran from the house (vv.10-12).

Mrs. Potiphar apparently didn't deal well with rejection. Proving that "Hell hath no fury like a woman scorned," she waved Joseph's shirt in the air and screamed until the servants came running. "He tried to rape me!" she sobbed. "I was saved only by my screams. He ran out, leaving his shirt behind" (vv. 14-15).

The servants bought her story. So did Potiphar. Furious, he took Joseph and threw him into Pharaoh's prison.

I don't know about you, but if I worked hard for an employer, did a great job, brought him outstanding success, and protected his interests with absolute integrity, I'd expect to be promoted, not imprisoned. Most likely, that's what Joseph expected too. But instead, he got blindsided—yet again. While his heart was still aching from his kinfolk's cruelty, his employer betrayed him too.

Once the devil had maneuvered Joseph into a jail cell, he must have thought for sure he'd finally put an end to the Dreamer and his divine dreams. But, once again, he was wrong.

Joseph kept his quiet, peaceful attitude...and God kept blessing him even in prison.

Before long, the jailer put Joseph in charge of all the other prisoners and over everything that happened in the prison. The chief jailer had no more worries after that, because Joseph took care of everything. The LORD was with him, making everything run smoothly and successfully (vv. 22-23).

ONE STUNNING QUESTION

"But Vikki," you might ask. "How can you be sure Joseph maintained a good attitude? Don't you think he got depressed about his situation and felt sorry for himself like anybody else would?"

No, I don't and here's why.

According to the Bible, one day during Joseph's stint in the slammer, he noticed a couple of other inmates looking dejected. "Why do you look so sad today?"[57] he said.

It sounds like a simple question. But you know as well as I do that if Joseph had been feeling sorry for himself he wouldn't have asked it. He wouldn't have cared how anybody else was feeling. He would have been too preoccupied with his own problems.

What's more, the way Joseph phrased his question indicates he saw no reason for feeling depressed—even though he'd been sold into slavery by his family and

---
[57] Genesis 40:7, NKJV

unjustly jailed by his employer. I can almost see Joseph's two fellow prisoners gaping at him with wide-eyed wonder and thinking, *Why do we look sad? Because we're in prison, that's why! We're locked up—possibly forever—with no idea whether we're going to live or die. And by the way, Joseph, so are you!*

Everyone in that prison must have marveled at the fact that Joseph could be so cheerful in the midst of such dismal circumstances.

What was his secret?

He kept his heart fixed on his divine dream. In spite of everything he'd been through, he kept on believing that God would fulfill His Word.

When Joseph's two gloomy friends (who also happened to be Pharaoh's servants) said they were worried about the dreams they'd each had the previous night, he assured them God would help them too. "Interpreting dreams is God's business," he said. "Tell me what you saw."[58] What amazing confidence!

In return for interpreting their dreams, Joseph asked for one simple favor. "Please have some pity on me when you go back to Pharaoh's palace," he said. "Mention me to him, and ask him to let me out of here. For I was kidnapped from my homeland, the land of the Hebrews, and now I'm here in jail but I did nothing to deserve it."[59]

Look again at that last sentence. Notice, Joseph said he was "kidnapped" from his homeland.

---

[58] v. 8
[59] vv. 14-15

He wasn't kidnapped! He was sold into slavery by his own brothers. Yet he refused to say anything about that. He wouldn't utter a single word of blame or bitterness against anyone.

Proverbs 10:12 says, "Hatred stirs up quarrels, but love covers all offenses." Joseph walked in love, so he graciously concealed the sins his family and his former employer had committed against him.

In the end, only one of Pharaoh's imprisoned servants ended up back in the palace...and he apparently forgot about Joseph. He neglected to put in a good word for him. Piling yet another betrayal on Joseph's plate, the servant left him unspoken for and locked up in jail for another two years.

> Joseph said he was "kidnapped" from his homeland. He wasn't kidnapped! He was sold into slavery by his own brothers. Yet he refused to say anything about that.

Try to remember that the next time somebody you've gone out of your way to help ignores you or treats you with ingratitude. Instead of getting mad at them, thank God that you're in good company. Like Joseph, you're just passing another detour on the way to the fulfillment of your dream. Such detours may not be pleasant. They may hurt. But if you'll guard your heart, if you'll keep it peaceful, quiet, and free from offense, when promotion day comes, you'll be ready.

Joseph certainly was. As Psalm 105 says:

> In prison, they bruised his feet with fetters and placed his neck in an iron collar. Until the time came to fulfill his word, the LORD tested Joseph's character. Then Pharaoh sent for him and set him free; the ruler of the nation opened his prison door. Joseph was put in charge of all the king's household; he became ruler over all the king's possessions. He could instruct the king's aides as he pleased and teach the king's advisers (vv. 18-22).

You probably know how it happened. Pharaoh had a dream that needed interpreting and (finally!) the servant remembered his prison encounter with Joseph. Pharaoh sent for Joseph, and he told Pharaoh that seven years of plenty in Egypt would be followed by seven years of famine. Then he proposed a plan to save the nation from starvation—a plan so wise it landed him the top spot in Pharaoh's administration.

And thus, Joseph became the leader and the deliverer God had promised him as a teenager he would be.

"Well, that's not how stories usually turn out in real life," somebody might argue. "People rarely see their dreams fulfilled in such a satisfying way."

Maybe that's because they don't pass the tests that Joseph did. Maybe they give in to bitterness and resentment when their family members, employers, or peers mistreat them. Maybe they let their flesh take control and choose the instant gratification of retaliation instead of waiting with patience for God's promises to manifest in their lives.

In other words, maybe they let the devil defuse their dreams.

I've heard it said that Joseph went from prisoner to Prime Minister overnight. But that's not really true. Joseph spent years preparing for that promotion. He guarded his heart and refused to return evil for evil. He worked hard to keep his heart peaceful and quiet so that he could always hear the still, small voice of God. That's why, when he got the opportunity to interpret Pharaoh's dream, he was able to do it.

That's why he fulfilled his destiny.

Once he stepped into that destiny, it could have been payback time. Joseph could have indulged in a little vengeance. When his brothers, facing starvation in their homeland, traveled to Egypt and literally bowed at his feet, begging to buy grain, they were completely at his mercy.

> It's said that Joseph went from prisoner to Prime Minister overnight. But that's not really true. Joseph spent years preparing for that promotion.

Talk about an opportunity to say, "I told you so!" Joseph could have had evened the score at that moment. He could have put them in prison, or required them to suffer in some other way for what they'd done to him.

But he didn't do it. On the contrary, he blessed them. He supplied their need for food, forgave them, and treated them with tenderness. As they trembled in fear before him, he said:

> "I am Joseph, your brother whom you sold into Egypt! But don't be angry with yourselves that you did this to me, for God did it! He sent me here ahead of you to preserve your lives... As far as I am concerned, God turned into good what you meant for evil, for he brought me to this high position I have today so that I could save the lives of many people. No, don't be afraid. Indeed, I myself will take care of you and your families." And he spoke very kindly to them, reassuring them (Genesis 45:4-5, 50:20-21 TLB).

Reading those verses, we might think Joseph's words of reconciliation came easily to him. But the reality is they came no easier to him than they do to us. Joseph didn't have a special DNA that made him immune to hurt. He felt all the same emotions that we feel. His flesh pressured him to lash out at those who'd offended him, just as ours does. He had to work, like anybody else, at keeping his heart free of bitterness. But he did it...and the reward he received was worth the effort.

DANGEROUSLY FAMILIAR TRAPS

I wish Joseph's story was entirely unique. I wish the rest of us had never experienced anything like what he did. But, of course, we do.

You already know that from experience. But even if you didn't, you could figure it out by reading through the Bible. Everybody in it who accomplished anything for God experienced mistreatment of one kind or another.

Including—and most especially—Jesus.

In previous chapters, we've already talked about how incessantly the religious leaders of His day harassed him. But they weren't his only persecutors. Jesus' family, like Joseph's, got in on the action too. They doubted and criticized Him. Even when He was working miracles and the crowds were thronging to hear Him preach, they refused to believe in Him. "He's out of his mind," they said.[60]

Sometimes even the people Jesus tried to minister to insulted Him. When He set out to preach in Samaria, for instance, the people there refused to have anything to do with Him. They wouldn't even let His disciples into the city. Their rejection made James and John (who were aptly called "the sons of thunder") so mad that "they said to Jesus, 'Lord, should we order down fire from heaven to burn them up?' But Jesus turned and rebuked them, and said, 'You do not know what manner of spirit you are of.'"[61]

---
[60] Mark 3:21
[61] Luke 9:54-55, NLT, NKJV

He refused to take offense.

Now and then, even the 12 disciples gave Jesus trouble. When He told them He would have to suffer and die on the cross, Peter actually rebuked Jesus. "Heaven forbid, Lord," he said. "This will never happen to you!"[62]

Once again, Jesus chose not to take Peter's rebuke personally. Instead, He identified the real author of and addressed the real purpose behind it. "Get away from me, Satan!" he said. "You are a dangerous trap to me. You are seeing things merely from a human point of view, and not from God's."[63]

The phrase "dangerous trap" comes from the Greek word *scandalon*. As we've already learned, it means *offense*. Peter wasn't intentionally being offensive. He didn't mean to be setting a dangerous trap for Jesus by tempting Him to focus on something other than the will of God. Like most of the people who throw offenses in our path, Peter was clueless.

Jesus, however, wasn't. He recognized Peter's comment for the *scandalon* it was, and chose not to take the bait.

---

[62] Matthew 16:22
[63] v. 23

That's the choice Jesus made every day of His life. Although offenses came at Him continually from all directions—from family, religious leaders, from people He reached out to bless, and even from His closest friends—Jesus refused to give in to them. He refused to let them disrupt His faith, dim His vision, or disturb the divine peace within Him. He lived His entire life on earth without becoming ensnared in Satan's traps because He always—always!—guarded His heart.

As His disciples, we can follow His example. We can live out the fulfillment of our God-given dreams by heeding, as Jesus did, the instructions in Proverbs 4:20-23:

> My son, pay attention to what I say; listen closely to my words. Do not let them out of your sight, keep them within your heart; for they are life to those who find them and health to a man's whole body. Above all else, guard your heart, for it is the wellspring of life (NIV).

DON'T LET AN HORS D' OEUVRE SPOIL THE MAIN COURSE

Notice those verses connect guarding your heart with keeping God's Word. That's because, when the devil comes after you with his strategies of offense, what he's actually trying to destroy is the Word that's inside you. He understands (probably far better than you do) just how much power that Word contains. He knows:

- It's the seed that grows up to "produce a huge harvest—thirty, sixty, or even a hundred times as much as had been planted."[64]
- It's the source of mountain-moving faith.
- It's the power that created the universe.
- It's the seed of the new birth.
- It's able to build you up and give you an inheritance in the Kingdom of God.
- It's the sword of the spirit you can use to cut the devil down to size and put him on the run.

No wonder the instant people hear the Word, "Satan cometh immediately, and taketh away the word that was sown in their hearts." No wonder he makes sure that "affliction or persecution ariseth for the word's sake [so that people get] offended."[65]

Offenses are not coincidental! They're meant to distract us from God's Word, because that Word is what empowers us to take ground for God's Kingdom.

And the more ground we take, the more ground the devil loses!

Is the Word really that important? you might wonder. *Would Satan really go to all that trouble just to get our attention off of it?*

Absolutely. Jesus made that clear the day He held a meeting at Martha's house. Do you remember what

---
[64] Mark 4:20
[65] vv. 15, 17 KJV

happened there? Martha didn't think she had time for the Word that day. She was too busy in the kitchen preparing dinner for the group that had come to hear Jesus speak. She was also preoccupied with—and mightily agitated by—the fact that her sister Mary, instead of helping her, was just sitting at Jesus' feet, listening to the Word as if there was nothing else to do.

For a while, Martha fumed in silence. But eventually, her agitation boiled over and she interrupted Jesus' message. "Master, don't you care that my sister has abandoned the kitchen to me?" she said, "Tell her to lend me a hand."

"Martha, dear Martha," Jesus answered, "you're fussing far too much and getting yourself worked up over nothing. One thing only is essential, and Mary has chosen it—it's the main course, and won't be taken from her."[66]

Don't make the mistake Martha did. Don't let the devil's hors d'oeuvres of agitation and offense distract you from God's main course of the Word.

> Self-reliance is downright dangerous—especially in times of trouble. The Apostle Paul even called it a *death sentence*.

If you do, you'll go spiritually hungry. You'll find yourself cut off from the supernatural guidance and delivering power that only God's Word can provide.

---

[66] Luke 10:41-42, MSG

You'll have nothing to depend on but your own natural reasoning and limited understanding.

Such self-reliance is downright dangerous—especially in times of trouble. The Apostle Paul even called it a *death sentence.* He said that in the worst times of his life, when people were literally trying to tear him apart, he'd learned that "we should not trust in ourselves but in God"[67]—the only One who truly has the power to deliver us in any situation.

TOO BIG A SACRIFICE TO MAKE

The Word isn't the only thing the devil is trying to steal from you. He's after something else as well: The anointing of God.

Although you may not think of yourself as especially anointed, the Bible says you are. It declares that as a born again child of God, "the anointing which you have received from Him abides in you."[68]

The devil is terrified of that anointing—and for good reason.

It has the power to absolutely obliterate his works. He can spend an entire lifetime loading somebody down with sin, sickness, and oppression, only to see all of it wiped out by the anointing in a split second. As Isaiah prophesied: "His burden shall be taken away from off thy shoulder, and his yoke from off thy neck, and the yoke shall be destroyed because of the anointing."[69]

---

[67] 2 Corinthians 1:9 NKJV
[68] 1 John 2:27
[69] Isaiah 10:27, KJV

It was the anointing that empowered Jesus during His ministry on earth to go "about doing good and healing all who were oppressed by the devil."[70] It was the anointing that enabled Him to "preach the gospel to the poor...to heal the brokenhearted, to proclaim liberty to the captives, and recovery of sight to the blind."[71] And it's the anointing that connects us with Jesus' miracle-working power today!

How does the devil go about stealing that anointing?

Look at what happened in Jesus' hometown and you'll see. When He went there to preach, instead of greeting Him with gladness like the multitudes in other places did, they got agitated at Him:

> They asked, "Where did he get all his wisdom and the power to perform such miracles? He's just the carpenter, the son of Mary and brother of James, Joseph, Judas, and Simon. And his sisters live right here among us." They were deeply offended and refused to believe in him (Mark 6:2-3).

Imagine it! They took offense at Jesus!

What happened as a result?

"He couldn't do any mighty miracles among them."[72] They were robbed of the power of His anointing.

As Christians, we might not take offense at Jesus in the same way the people in Nazareth did; but here's

---
[70] Acts 10:38, NKJV
[71] Luke 4:17, NKJV
[72] v. 5

the reality: Offense of any kind, directed at anybody, can block God's supernatural intervention in the affairs of our life. That's why Jesus took it so seriously.

He went so far as to say, "if thine eye offend thee, pluck it out."[73]

None of us will ever have to follow those instructions in the literal sense. But even so, we need to remember how much offense can cost us. We need to be determined to pluck it out of our hearts the moment it tries to take root in us, because it will rob us of the power of the anointing. It will hinder our healing, block our financial breakthroughs, mar our marriage, and keep our children from turning to God.

In other words, it will stop us from receiving the miracles we need in our lives. And no matter how we've been hurt, no matter who has done us wrong, that's too big a sacrifice to make.

> Offense of any kind, directed at anybody, can block God's supernatural intervention in the affairs of our life. That's why Jesus took it so seriously.

---
[73] Matthew 18:9, KJV

8

WHEN LIFE DISAPPOINTS YOU

Then saith Jesus unto them, All ye shall be offended because of me this night...Peter answered and said unto him, Though all men shall be offended because of thee, yet will I never be offended. Jesus said unto him, Verily I say unto thee, That this night, before the cock crow, thou shalt deny me thrice. Peter said unto him, Though I should die with thee, yet will I not deny thee. Likewise also said all the disciples.
Matthew 26:31,33-35

I don't mean to contradict myself, but I want to clarify a remark I made in the last chapter. When I said that we, as contemporary Christians, might not take offense at Jesus the same way the people in Nazareth did, I was being overly optimistic. The plain truth is, at one time or another, most of us do.

Our reasons are a little different than theirs were, of course. They got offended at Jesus because of how *normal* He was. They'd spent a lifetime imagining their Messiah as a man of mythical proportions—as a king like David with a mighty army, or a prophet like Elijah calling fire down from heaven. So when Jesus told them He was the One they'd been waiting for, they were really upset.

How could their great Deliverer be simply a grown up version of the hometown kid they'd seen all their lives? How could the baby Mary carried around on her hip, the youngster that played games with the neighborhood kids, have somehow become the Savior of Israel?

> They got offended at Jesus because of how *normal* He was. They'd spent a lifetime imagining their Messiah as a man of mythical proportions.

The very idea so shocked and disappointed the population of Nazareth that when Jesus came and taught in their synagogue: "They were deeply offended and refused to believe in him" (Mark 6:3).

Those of us who live a couple of thousand years after the resurrection often gasp at that concept. We shake our heads as if we can't imagine getting upset with Jesus for any reason at all. We forget how we sometimes react when we are disappointed with God.

Don't sit there looking all innocent. You know what I'm talking about. We've all been tempted at times to get mad at Him when things didn't turn out the way we wanted. Maybe we thought we were going to get a promotion at work...and got laid off instead. Maybe we prayed for someone to be healed...and they died. Maybe we hit a trying season of life, begged God to deliver us from it immediately...and instead that season dragged on and on.

How did we react to such situations? Did we ever feel anything like the people in Nazareth did? Disappointed? Shocked? Angry? Upset?

"Well, I might have been disappointed," somebody might say, "but I wasn't deeply offended. And I certainly didn't stop believing in Jesus because of it. I'd never do that!"

Really?

You might want to check with Apostle Peter before you make that assertion. He once said the same thing. Less than 48 hours before he totally denied Jesus, he boasted with great boldness, "Though all men shall be offended because of thee, yet will I never be offended."[74]

Never mind that Jesus had told His disciples just seconds earlier that they would all be offended because of Him that night. Peter knew better! His devotion to the Lord would never waver, no matter what happened. He was confident of it.

Why shouldn't he be? He'd already proven his commitment to Jesus. He'd left everything to follow Him. Turning his back on his home, his fishing business, and his place in the community, he'd become a

---
[74] Matthew 26:31,33, KJV

disciple without receiving a single guarantee from the Lord about his future.

Peter was also one of Jesus' closest friends. A part of His most trusted ministry team, Peter was with Him on the Mount of Transfiguration when Elijah and Moses appeared. On the Sea of Galilee, Peter had been the only one bold enough to step out of the boat and walk to Jesus on the water. In the Garden of Gethsemane, the night before the crucifixion, he was one of the three disciples Jesus invited to pray with Him.

> When the soldiers showed up in Gethsemane, accompanied by a torch-toting, sword-carrying, club-swinging mob bent on arresting Jesus and putting Him to death, Peter dared to defend Him.

If those things weren't evidence enough of his unwavering loyalty, when the soldiers showed up in Gethsemane, accompanied by a torch-toting, sword-carrying, club-swinging mob bent on arresting Jesus and putting Him to death, Peter dared to defend Him. He "drew a sword and slashed off the right ear of Malchus, the high priest's servant."[75]

Peter wasn't really aiming for the ear. He was just a lousy swordsman. He'd spent his life baiting hooks, not doing battle. But he was willing to fight anyway, and even die for Jesus, because he loved Him so much.

---

[75] John 18:10

Does that sound like the kind of man who would fall prey to offense and unbelief?

No, it doesn't.

Which proves that if it can happen to Peter, it can happen to anybody—including me and you.

EXACTLY WHO BETRAYED WHOM?

Considering our mutual vulnerability, we'd be wise to find out what it was that tripped Peter up. What changed him in just a matter of hours from a sword-wielding believer to a cowardly denier?

Things didn't go the way he expected in the Garden of Gethsemane.

When the soldier came to arrest Jesus, Peter expected Him to intervene in some supernatural way. He assumed His miracle-working Lord would do something amazing. That He'd put the rabble rousers to shame, and walk away from the situation, along with His disciples, triumphant and unharmed.

After all, Jesus had done that kind of thing time and again. He'd once walked right through the middle of a raging mob intent on killing Him, and they weren't even able to touch Him. He'd fearlessly faced down and delivered a madman so demon-possessed that even chains couldn't hold him. He'd subdued a raging sea. Fed a hungry multitude with a little boy's lunch.

Peter had witnessed it all. He knew full well there was no problem too big for Jesus to handle, no challenge or opposition too great for Him to overcome.

So that's what Peter expected Him to do that night in Gethsemane.

Overcome.

Overcome the soldiers and the religious leaders. Overcome the swords and the clubs. Stand His ground and defeat them like He'd defeated every other evil thing for the past three years.

But instead, Jesus did the unthinkable. The unimaginable. He rebuked Peter for defending Him. Rather than commending him for his courage, He said "Put away your sword...Those who use the sword will be killed by the sword. Don't you realize that I could ask my Father for thousands of angels to protect us, and he would send them instantly?"[76]

Yes, I do realize that, Peter must have thought. *So why don't You do it? Why don't You call an angel army right now, end this thing, and take Your place as King?*

"If I did, how would the Scriptures be fulfilled...?"[77] Jesus said.

Shocked and confused, Peter—for once—was speechless. All he could do was stare, mute with horror, as Jesus surrendered and let the soldiers take Him away.

Fleeing the scene with the other disciples, terrified that he'd be arrested too, Peter's mind must have been racing. *What just happened? Why did Jesus suddenly change His way of doing things? I left everything for Him! I gave up my whole life—for what?! So that I could be part*

---

[76] Matthew 26:51-52
[77] v. 54

of short-lived fantasy that ends in defeat? Now what am I supposed to do?

Because we usually think of Peter as the one who betrayed Jesus, we rarely consider this: At that moment in Gethsemane, Peter felt like Jesus was betraying him. The way he saw it, Jesus was walking out on His commitments; He was breaking His promises; He was abandoning His disciples and giving up everything they'd fought for.

Peter felt hurt, disappointed, and deeply offended.

Just like the people at Nazareth did.

Just like we sometimes do, when things don't go like we expect and our world seems to come crashing down around us.

WHAT'S BEHIND THE FEAR?

The Bible makes it clear, Jesus warned Peter about what was coming. Earlier that day, He'd given him a chilling prophetic word: "Peter...the truth is, this very night, before the rooster crows, you will deny me three times."[78]

Within hours, His words came true.

While Jesus was being accused, spit upon, slapped, and beaten in the house of the high priest, Peter was sitting outside in the courtyard when a servant girl came over and said to him,

> "You were one of those with Jesus the Galilean."

---

[78] v. 34

Peter denied it in front of everyone. "I don't know what you are talking about," he said.

Later, out by the gate, another servant girl noticed him and said to those standing around, "This man was with Jesus of Nazareth."

Again Peter denied it, this time with an oath. "I don't even know the man," he said.

A little later some other bystanders came over to him and said, "You must be one of them; we can tell by your Galilean accent."

Peter said, "I swear by God, I don't know the man." And immediately the rooster crowed. Suddenly, Jesus' words flashed through Peter's mind: "Before the rooster crows, you will deny me three times." And he went away, crying bitterly (Matthew 26:69-75).

> Like a tempest on the Sea of Galilee, the winds of disappointment and the waves of offense had sunk Peter's faith.

Have you ever really thought about what was going on inside Peter during that interaction?

Sure, he was scared, but what was behind his fear? Why was he suddenly so afraid to admit that he knew Jesus?

Because, although he knew Him, he'd stopped believing in Him.

Like a tempest on the Sea of Galilee, the winds of disappointment and the waves of offense had sunk Peter's faith.

That's what always happens when people get offended at God. Think again about the people in Nazareth. "They were deeply offended *and refused to believe...*"[79]

That's the devil's agenda. It's the whole reason he comes after us in such situations, pushing us to ask, "Why, Lord? Why?" He wants to destroy our faith, because faith is what connects us to God.

This may surprise you, but the devil isn't nearly as interested in making us stumble on the outside as he is in making us doubt on the inside. He isn't as interested in our behavior as he is in our believing. The reason is simple: It's not our good behavior that saves us; it's what we believe. As Jesus said, "God so loved the world that he gave his only Son, so that everyone who *believes in him* will not perish but have eternal life."[80]

The opposite is also true. "He who does not believe is condemned...because he has not believed in the name of the only begotten Son of God."[81]

Just as good behavior doesn't get people into heaven, bad behavior isn't what keeps them out. They aren't condemned because they smoke, drink, use foul language, or engage in immorality. The penalty for those things was paid on the cross. The only sin left that the cross cannot cover is rejecting the Savior.

---

[79] Mark 6:3
[80] John 3:16
[81] v. 17

"The world's sin is unbelief in me," Jesus said. "If anyone acknowledges me publicly here on earth, I will openly acknowledge that person before my Father in heaven. But if anyone denies me here on earth, I will deny that person before my Father in heaven."[82]

Refusing to believe in Jesus as Savior and Lord, denying who He is and what He's done, has eternal consequences. The Bible confirms it again and again. Using the strongest possible terms it says:

> And who is the great liar? The one who says that Jesus is not the Christ. Such people are antichrists, for they have denied the Father and the Son. Anyone who denies the Son doesn't have the Father either. But anyone who confesses the Son has the Father also (1 John 2:22-23).

Many mistakes can be forgiven, but permanently denying the deity of Jesus is not one of them.

FROM A PICNIC IN THE PARK TO A FIERY TRIAL OF FAITH

"But I'm already a Christian!" you might say. "I'm never going to deny Jesus is the Son of God. I'm not going to reject Him as my Redeemer and Lord."

No, you probably won't. But that doesn't mean the devil will stop trying to get you to doubt. No matter how committed a Christian you may be, he will still attack you when the events of life don't turn out like

---
[82] John, 16:9, Matthew 10:32-33

you expect. Tempting you to question God's faithfulness and His Word, he'll try to get you offended so that he can steal at least a portion of your faith.

I've seen it happen. One woman I know was an enthusiastic believer and even worked for a ministry until she got the idea that God was going to give her a new house within 30 days. She'd given an offering as a seed of faith for it, and she was sure she'd receive a harvest right away.

I warned her that God doesn't always work on our timetable, but she ignored me. Thinking she was acting in faith, she notified the manager of her apartment that she'd be leaving the next month. As you might guess, she didn't get her new house in time. She was forced to move because her apartment had been rented to someone else. Blaming God for failing to come through for her, she wound up quitting her job with the ministry and walking away from the Lord.

> We think we've figured out how certain situations are going to go, only to be shocked when they take an entirely different (and sometimes difficult) turn.

Although that's an extreme example, most of us can identify with it. We know what it's like to think we've figured out how certain situations are going to go, only to be shocked when they take an entirely different (and sometimes difficult) turn. We've all felt the hurt and disappointment that come when we think God has promised us a picnic in the park and we find ourselves in the midst of a fiery trial instead.

Even the great New Testament prophet, John the Baptist, had that experience. Like Peter, he expected Jesus to defeat evil and take the throne of Israel in his lifetime. He expected Jesus to come on the scene roaring like a lion, not laying down His life like a lamb. John thought Jesus would reveal His identity to the entire world the way God had revealed it to him when, baptizing Jesus in the Jordan, "suddenly a voice came from heaven, saying, "This is My beloved Son, in whom I am well pleased."[83]

But it never happened.

Jesus threw John a curve. He didn't operate exactly as he expected. Not only was He meek and nonpolitical, when Herod put John in prison Jesus didn't even show up to demand his release. Sitting behind bars, waiting to be executed, doubts began to cloud John's mind. His faith in the Word he'd heard from heaven began to waver.

So he sent his disciples to ask Jesus, "Are you really the Messiah we've been waiting for, or should we keep looking for someone else?"

> Jesus told them, "Go back to John and tell him about what you have heard and seen—the blind see, the lame walk, the lepers are cured, the deaf hear, the dead are raised to life, and

---

[83] Matthew 3:17, NKJ

the Good News is being preached to the poor. And tell him: 'God blesses those who are not offended by me'" (Matthew 11:2-6).

If anybody had reason to be offended at Jesus, John did. His prophetic ministry appeared to be ending in a way he never envisioned. His Messiah had disappointed him by refusing to set up an earthly kingdom. And he couldn't understand why.

John had some major questions. Yet even so, Jesus told him to keep the faith. He said, in essence, "John, don't allow what you don't understand to disconnect you from Me. You heard what God said at the Jordan. Keep believing it."

He says the same to us when we're tempted to let our disappointing circumstances cause us to question God's character and integrity. He reminds us that, although there's a lot we don't yet understand, we can be assured of this: God has never failed anyone and He never will. He's faithful to His people, faithful to His Word, and nothing can separate us from His love. If we'll stay hooked up to Him and believe what He said, we'll end up more blessed than we ever dreamed we could be.

But if we get offended and begin to doubt Him, it will cost us dearly.

STOP ASKING WHY AND START ASKING WHO

How can we be certain we won't have to pay that cost? How can we prepare ourselves so that when life deals us an unexpected blow we won't get upset with God?

We can learn the lessons that Peter provided. We can look at how he put himself in danger and benefit from his mistakes.

His first blunder was failing to pay attention to Jesus' warnings. He should have taken seriously what the Lord said to him and the other disciples about being offended that night. But he didn't. He just shrugged off Jesus' words and decided they didn't apply to him.

Thank God, we don't have to follow that example. We can choose to believe and heed the many warnings Jesus gave us in the Bible:

- Woe to the world because of offenses! For offenses must come, but woe to that man by whom the offense comes! (Matthew 18:7, KJV).
- Many will be offended, will betray one another, and will hate one another (Matthew 24:10, NKJV).
- And these are they likewise which are sown on stony ground; who, when they have heard the word, immediately receive it with gladness; And...afterward, when affliction or persecution ariseth for the word's sake, immediately they are offended (Mark 4:16-17, NKJV).
- It is impossible that no offenses should come... (Luke 17:1, NKJV).
- These things have I spoken unto you, that ye should not be offended (John 16:1, KJV).

If we pay attention to those warnings, we'll be more apt to guard our hearts by keeping them full of the Word. We'll also stay more attuned to the promptings of the Holy Spirit. He lives on the inside of us and part of His job is to prepare us for what's to come.[84] If we'll be sensitive to Him, He'll alert us in advance so that we'll be ready when the storms of life try to rock our boat.

Those storms are coming, you know. As Peter found out, you're not always going to have smooth sailing just because you're a faithful disciple of Jesus. And as my friend who expected a new house in 30 days found out, God won't always do everything you want Him to do on your schedule.

Don't misunderstand me. I'm not saying you can't trust God to keep His Word.

You can!

I'm not saying He won't keep all His promises to you.

He will!

I'm just saying that sometimes you'll have to stand in faith before those promises manifest.

Peter eventually learned that lesson so well that he wrote about it in the New Testament.

> "Dear friends," he said, "don't be surprised at the fiery trials you are going through, as if something strange were happening to you.

---

[84] John 16:13: When He, the Spirit of truth, has come, He will guide you into all truth; for He will not speak on His own authority, but whatever He hears He will speak; and He will tell you things to come.

Instead, be very glad—because these trials will make you partners with Christ in his suffering, and afterward you will have the wonderful joy of sharing his glory when it is displayed to all the world....So be truly glad! There is wonderful joy ahead, even though it is necessary for you to endure many trials for a while. These trials are only to test your faith, to show that it is strong and pure. It is being tested as fire tests and purifies gold—and your faith is far more precious to God than mere gold. So if your faith remains strong after being tried by fiery trials, it will bring you much praise and glory and honor on the day when Jesus Christ is revealed to the whole world (1 Peter 4:12-13, 1:6-7).

One thing you might want to remember is that our faith isn't always tried in our strongest area. The devil often targets our weaknesses. Like a linebacker blindsiding a quarterback, he hits us when and where we least expect it. So we can never afford to let down our guard in any area of life.

If you do happen to get blindsided, don't respond like Peter did. When the devil knocked the wind out of him, he ran away from the people he needed most. He disconnected from the other disciples and followed Jesus "at a distance."[85] He let the question *Why did this happen?* drive a wedge between him and the very Source of his faith.

---

[85] Luke 22:54, NKJ

When you find yourself falling into that trap, stop asking *why* and start asking *who?* Get your eyes off your disappointments and onto the One who can get you through them. The One who will always love you and keep His promises to you. The One who will never leave you nor forsake you.

> Like a linebacker blindsiding a quarterback, he hits us when and where we least expect it. So we can never afford to let down our guard in any area of life.

If you'll stop asking, *Why did this happen?* and start asking, *Who should I turn to?* you'll get the answer that will take you in the right direction.

Jesus.

And instead of following Him at a distance, you'll run straight into His arms.

JESUS CAN MAKE THINGS RIGHT AGAIN

"But what if I've already doubted and denied Him?" you might ask. "What if I've already fallen into the devil's trap? Can Jesus do anything for me?"

Oh, yes.

That's the best thing about Peter's story. It has a great ending because Jesus was there for him from first to last. He knew in advance Peter wasn't going to listen to His warnings, so He backed him up in prayer. "Simon, Simon," he said, "Satan has asked to have all of you, to sift you like wheat. But I have pleaded in prayer for you, Simon, that your faith should not fail. So when you have repented and turned to me again, strengthen and build up your brothers."[86]

Would Jesus pray that kind of prayer for you?

Without a doubt.

The Bible says "He always lives to make intercession" for those of us who come to God through Him.[87]

Talk about having a mighty prayer warrior on your side! The Lord Jesus Himself is interceding for you. And if you stumble and fall, He'll help you get back on your feet.

> Talk about having a mighty prayer warrior on your side! The Lord Jesus Himself is interceding for you. And He'll help you get back on your feet.

Peter found that out in a beautiful way. He was grief stricken after he denied Jesus. Certain he no longer qualified as a disciple, he went back to his fishing business, devastated, ashamed, and alone.

But Jesus came to get him and make things right again.

The morning it happened, Peter and the other disciples had been out on the lake fishing all night without catching anything.

> At dawn the disciples saw Jesus standing on the beach, but they couldn't see who he was.

---
[86] Luke 22:31-32
[87] Hebrews 7:25, NKJ

He called out, "Friends, have you caught any fish?" "No," they replied. Then he said, "Throw out your net on the right-hand side of the boat, and you'll get plenty of fish!" So they did, and they couldn't draw in the net because there were so many fish in it. Then the disciple whom Jesus loved said to Peter, "It is the Lord!" When Simon Peter heard that it was the Lord, he put on his tunic (for he had stripped for work), jumped into the water, and swam ashore (John 21:4-7).

I'm sure that even though Peter was eager to see Jesus, his heart was still troubled by the memory of his denials. *Will the Lord ever really believe that I love Him?* he must have wondered. *Will He ever be able to trust me again?*

For a while, Jesus didn't address his questions. He didn't even mention what Peter had done. He just said, "Bring some of the fish you've caught, and come have breakfast!"

Then, after breakfast, Jesus put Peter's mind to rest. He said:

> "Simon son of John, do you love me more than these?"
>
> "Yes, Lord," Peter replied, "you know I love you."
>
> "Then feed my lambs," Jesus told him. Jesus repeated the question: "Simon son of John, do

> you love me?" "Yes, Lord," Peter said, "you know I love you."
>
> "Then take care of my sheep," Jesus said. Once more he asked him, "Simon son of John, do you love me?"
>
> Peter was grieved that Jesus asked the question a third time. He said, "Lord, you know everything. You know I love you."
>
> Jesus said, "Then feed my sheep" (vv. 15-17).

People often point out that in this conversation Jesus gave Peter the opportunity to replace his three denials with three declarations of love. While that's true, and very precious, there's something else about it I find even more significant.

Jesus asked Peter to do Him a favor.

You don't ask people to do you a favor unless you trust them. Especially if that favor involves something important and dear to your heart. And in this case, it definitely did. Jesus was asking Peter to carry out the ministry that He Himself had begun. He was giving him the greatest possible vote of confidence by entrusting into his care the lambs for whom He'd laid down His life.

Jesus' request must have rung like music in Peter's ears. It assured him that Jesus hadn't disowned him. He hadn't set him aside.

From that day on, Peter was free from condemnation. He knew he was forgiven and redeemed.

He spent the rest of his life carrying out the commission he'd been given. And, even when his faith was tested through "fiery trials," he refused to question what he didn't understand. Having learned his lesson, he kept his eyes on the Who instead of the why, and he never doubted Jesus again.

NEXT TIME YOU CAN BE PREPARED

No matter how hard you may have fallen in the past, you can get back up and finish the way Peter did. You can stop following Jesus from afar and draw near to Him again. Reaching deep inside your heart, you can decide to put your life in His hands once and for all, believing He knows what He's doing and He'll never fail you or make a mistake.

> No matter how hard you may have fallen in the past, you can get back up and finish the way Peter did.

Then, the next time some circumstance of life disappoints you, you'll be prepared to handle it. You'll be able to say, "I don't understand what's going on, Lord, but I know You're faithful, righteous, just, and good. I trust You. I believe in You. Even though I'm hurting, I will not deny You."

Instead of questioning God and pulling away from Him, you'll be able to follow the instructions He gave us in the Bible:

"Trust in the LORD with all your heart, and lean not on your own understanding; In all your ways acknowledge Him, and He shall direct your paths."[88]

---

[88] Proverbs 3:5-6, NKJ

9

IT'S TIME TO PLAY SOME SERIOUS OFFENSE

*Remember that in a race everyone runs,
but only one person gets the prize.
You also must run in such a way that
you will win.*
1 Corinthians 9:24

I'm not a football fan or a betting woman either. But if I were I'd never put my money on a team that just plays defense.

That kind of team can't win.

In football, as in life, winners always have an offensive strategy. They know where the goal is and they're prepared to go after it. They have an aggressive game plan.

Sadly, most Christians don't. That's why they're often defeated by the devil. They show up on the spiritual playing field expecting to become champions, with only the vaguest idea of how to do it. Naïve as Pop Warner players on the first day of practice, they think that just because they're saved and God loves them, everything's going to turn out right.

It's a good thing their lives aren't televised. I can only imagine what they might say in a pre-game interview.

Commentator: So what's it going to take to outscore the devil tonight?

Christian: I don't know. I'm just going try to stay out of his way and hope he doesn't hurt me.

Commentator: He is definitely a serious, hard-hitting player. Have you spent any extra hours in the gym or on the practice field getting ready for this game?

> In football, as in life, winners always have an offensive strategy. They know where the goal is and they're prepared to go after it.

Christian: I'm not sure where the gym and practice field are located, so I've never been there. But I'm on the team and have a jersey with Jesus' name on it. I'm counting on that to be enough.

Commentator: Are you saying you haven't worked out or practiced any plays, and you're still expecting to make it across the goal line?

Christian (whispering): I've been meaning to ask about that. Exactly what is a goal line?

Okay, I'm joking. But this is a serious reality. Too many Christians spend their entire lives playing defense to the devil's offense. They never make much progress in life because he's scoring all the points and they're just trying to survive.

Don't get me wrong. It's not that defense isn't important. It is. It's is a vital part of spiritual victory, and thus far it's been the primary focus of this book. The Bible says, "Resist the Devil;"[89] and that's mostly what we've been learning to do.

But resistance by itself won't make you a winner. It won't propel you into God's great plan for your life. To do that, you have to go on the offensive. You have to run toward the end zone, knocking demons out of your way, and fulfilling your divine call.

Like the Apostle Paul, you have to get spiritually aggressive enough to say, "This one thing I do, forgetting those things which are behind, and reaching forth unto those things which are before, I press toward the mark for the prize of the high calling of God in Christ Jesus."[90]

Pressing takes spiritual muscle. It involves training and preparation. It requires us to be proactive. We don't *press* by just sitting around watching American Idol, eating nachos, and waiting for the devil's next attack. We can't advance toward our spiritual mark if we open our Bible only when we've been mistreated and we're trying to fend off an onslaught of hurt.

---

[89] James 4:7
[90] Philippians 3:13-14, KJV

If we live like that, we'll fold when the pressure hits. We'll not only fail to gain any ground, we'll find ourselves going backward. Responding to the devil's offensive plays by calling all our friends and begging them to pray for us, we'll end up doing the very things we know we shouldn't. We'll get mad. Get hurt. And say something stupid.

> We can't advance toward our spiritual mark if we open our Bible only when we've been mistreated and we're trying to fend off an onslaught of hurt.

In other words, we'll wind up taking the low road. How do I know that?

Because as spiritual beings, we're wired to go into "automatic" when a crisis hits. Our minds are designed to take a back seat to our spirit in times of emergency. God created us that way so that instead of falling apart or depending on our own limited understanding, we'd access the wisdom and Word of God within us and come through every trouble in triumph.

Proverbs 20:5 says, "Counsel in the heart of man is like deep water; but a man of understanding will draw it out." That's what we're designed to do when crunch time comes—draw out of our heart the counsel (advice, plans, purposes, and wisdom) of God.

It's an awesome system. There's just one hitch: For the Word to come out of us at such times, it must already be in us. Which means we don't want to wait till we've got the ball in our hands and the devil breathing down our neck to ask, "Now, what does the Bible say I'm supposed to do with this thing?"

That's a good way to lose the game.

I know I'm leaning hard on the sports metaphor, but it's absolutely scriptural. In his New Testament letters, Paul repeatedly compared the Christian life to an athletic competition. Using the various Roman sports of his era to drive home his points, he said:

- Remember that in a race everyone runs, but only one person gets the prize. You also must run in such a way that you will win. All athletes practice strict self-control. They do it to win a prize that will fade away, but we do it for an eternal prize. So I run straight to the goal with purpose in every step. I am not like a boxer who misses his punches. I discipline my body like an athlete, training it to do what it should (1 Corinthians 9:24-27).
- Let us strip off every weight that slows us down, especially the sin that so easily hinders our progress. And let us run with endurance the race that God has set before us (Hebrews 12:1-2).
- For we wrestle...against powers, against the rulers of the darkness of this world, against spiritual wickedness in high places (Ephesians 6:12, KJV).

- Follow the Lord's rules for doing his work, just as an athlete either follows the rules or is disqualified and wins no prize (2 Timothy 2:5).
- I have fought a good fight, I have finished the race, and I have remained faithful. And now the prize awaits me—the crown of righteousness that the Lord, the righteous Judge, will give me on that great day of his return. And the prize is not just for me but for all who eagerly look forward to his glorious return (2 Timothy 4:7-8).

DEVELOP THE HABITS OF A WINNER

Football wasn't being played in Paul's day, but if it were, I think he would have talked about making tackles and touchdowns. Coaching us like a Lombardi, he even might have given a Biblical version of this famous quote:

> You don't win once in a while, you don't do things right once in a while, you do them right all the time. Winning is a habit. Unfortunately, so is losing.

Winning is not a sometime thing; it's an all time thing. You don't win once in a while, you don't do things right once in a while, you do them right all the time. Winning is a habit. Unfortunately, so is losing.[91]

---

[91] Vince Lombardi, long time coach of the Green bay Packers

That's as true for believers as it is for athletes. If we're going to beat the devil and walk in our destiny, we have to do what's right all the time. We have to develop the habits of a spiritual winner.

The most important of those habits is spending time in God's Word every day.

Why is daily time in the Word so crucial?

Because it's our spiritual food. It's what nourishes and strengthens our inner man. It's what helps us grow up in the Lord.

We all start out in the Christian life as spiritual babies—weak, helpless, and clueless. That's okay for a while. After all, babies are great! As parents, we love our sweet little babies, don't we? But when they get to be 20 or 30 years old and they're still acting like infants, we want to slap them and say, "Grow up!"

The same is true in the Kingdom of God. Infancy is fine if it doesn't last too long. But some believers let it drag on for years.

They keep thinking they're going to mature automatically over time, but it never happens because that's not how things work. We don't become spiritual grownups just because we've been saved for a decade or two. We have to feed on the truths of the Bible. We have to do what First Peter 2:2 says and, "As newborn babes, desire the sincere milk of the word, that ye may grow thereby."[92]

Personally, I enjoy growing. It improves my life. When I look back at how much Jesus has done for me

---

[92] KJV

over the years as I've grown in Him, I want to grow even more. I not only want to keep drinking the milk of the Word (that's the easy stuff God tells us to do), I want chow down on the meat. I want to eat the solid food that, as Hebrews 5:14 says, "is for those who are mature, who have trained themselves to recognize the difference between right and wrong and then do what is right."

Notice, according to that verse, if we don't want to be stuck eating spiritual pabulum all our lives, we have to train ourselves. The word *train* means *to develop or form habits, thoughts, or behavior by discipline or instruction, to make fit by vigorous exercise, to bring into a desired form or direction by obedience.*

Bible knowledge without training won't get us anywhere. The Pharisees in the Gospels proved that. They were experts when it came to studying the Bible, yet Jesus continually had to rebuke them. "You search the Scriptures because you believe they give you eternal life," He said, "but the Scriptures point to me! Yet you refuse to come to me so that I can give you this eternal life."[93]

The Pharisees knew the Word but they didn't apply it. They refused to live what they'd learned.

People do that in a lot of different areas. Take exercise, for instance. Some people watch videos and read books about it. They buy the clothes and equipment. Yet their muscles stay weak and scrawny, their bellies big and doughy, because they never actually train.

---
[93] John 5:39-40

I understand those people. You probably do too. We know from experience that training, because it involves overcoming resistance, isn't any fun. That's why, from time to time, we go to the gym, lift a barbell a few times, and suddenly start thinking, *What am I doing here? I don't want to lift this thing. It hurts. This is too hard. My body doesn't really look that bad.*

Then we go home and collapse on the couch.

You may not consider this especially good news, but spiritual training is much like physical training. Just as we build up our outward man by lifting weights, we build up our inward man by the resistance of our flesh. We pump up our spiritual muscles by "putting to death the deeds of the body,"[94] and doing what God tells us to do—whether it's keeping our mouth shut when somebody makes us mad, responding with love when somebody treats us ugly, or doing a good job at work even though the boss doesn't appreciate us.

> Just as we build up our outward man by lifting weights, we build up our inward man by the resistance of our flesh.

Those things aren't fun. But as we've already seen, our destinies depend on them. And, like Lombardi said, if we want to make sure we do them when it really counts, we must do them all the time. We must discipline ourselves to do what's right every day in

---
[94] Romans 8:13, NASB

the minor issues of life when it doesn't it look like it matters, so that we won't blow it when something major happens and our future is on the line.

Proverbs 22:6 puts it this way. "Train up a child in the way he should go: and when he is old, he will not depart from it." Or, paraphrasing it to fit this context, *Train up yourself in the way you should go: and when you're under pressure, you will not depart from it.*

The Hebrew word translated *train* in that scripture doesn't mean what you might expect. It doesn't refer to teaching or discipline. It refers to the way Israelite babies were weaned in Old Testament times. Back then, Gerber's wasn't around yet, so a mother would take a bite of food and chew it until it was soft enough for her baby to eat. Then she'd take it out of her mouth and put it on his palette. As she repeated this process over and over with a various kinds of solid foods, the child would develop a taste for them.

It sounds disgusting, I'll admit. But even so, it's a good picture of the process we believers go through as we to grow to maturity.

When we're babies, the things God tells us to do in His Word don't always appeal to us. They're hard on our flesh and they don't suit our immature spiritual appetites. But they're right and they're good for us. So we keep feeding on that Word and putting it into practice. Over time, our palettes mature and we develop a taste for doing God's will.

PRACTICE MAKES BETTER

One translation of Hebrews 5:14 substitutes the word practice for training. It says, "the mature...*because of practice* have their senses trained to discern good and evil."[95]

In any endeavor that requires skill, practice is essential. My daughter, Jessica, learned that as a kid watching Sesame Street. One of the program's characters—a man who played the piano—frequently sang a song that went something like this: "Practice, practice, do it again, over and over till you get it. Practice, practice, learn how to play..."

When Jessica started taking piano lessons, that song came in especially handy. I used it to encourage her to practice every day. I never had to nag her because, even as a little girl, she understood that practice would make her proficient.

Look again at that last word. It's *proficient*, not *perfect*.

The old saying, *Practice makes perfect*, is a lie. If practice made people perfect, Olympic athletes, who spend most of their waking hours for four years practicing their sport, would always perform to perfection in the Olympic Games. But they don't. They often make mistakes.

So do we. So if you're a perfectionist, please relax. Quit expecting yourself to be a flawless Christian. You're setting yourself up for failure. No matter how

---
[95] NASB

hard you try, you'll still mess up sometimes. You'll still stumble, because practice doesn't make you perfect.

Practice makes you better.

Knowing that takes the pressure off, doesn't it? It gives us more freedom to grow. Instead of wanting to give up on our spiritual training every time we fail, we can just repent, receive God's forgiveness, and get back up again. We can be like the Olympians. When they make mistakes, they don't get discouraged and walk away. They say, "I'll keep training. I'll go after it and be back in another four years!"

> If you're a perfectionist, please relax. Quit expecting yourself to be a flawless Christian. You're setting yourself up for failure.

Granted, it's not always easy for us to take that attitude. It's tempting to get frustrated and start comparing ourselves to others who are ahead of us in some area. We might look at how they've disciplined their flesh or how patient and loving they are, and think, *I'll never get there! Why should I even try? What's the point?*

The point is we're working on it! And if we'll keep working on it, we'll keep getting better.

Spiritual growth, like physical growth, is gradual. We don't just decide we're going to do this and become mature in a day. We increase a little at a time, as the Bible says, from faith to faith and from glory to glory.

"For precept must be upon precept...line upon line, here a little, and there a little."[96]

Do you remember when you were a kid and your parents made pencil marks on the wall to track your growth from month to month and year to year? You got excited about every new mark, didn't you? You didn't get frustrated over the fact that you weren't completely "grown." You celebrated your progress.

You can do the same thing spiritually. You can track your growth by marking your attitude toward mistreatment. The more you respond with love, patience, and restraint when others do you wrong, the more progress you're making. The more mature you're becoming. And that's worth celebrating because with maturity comes freedom.

When you're a spiritual grownup, people can mistreat you, but they can't control you. Nobody can make you mad. No one can steal your destiny. You're free.

And that's a very fun way to live.

ADVANCE THE BALL BY SPEAKING THE WORD

A daily diet of the Word, accompanied by training and practice, will go a long way toward taking us from Pee Wee to Pro in our Christian life. But there's something else we have to do too. If we want to finish this game like champions, we must get out there on the field and actually play offense. We must execute the scriptural strategies that will flatten our opposition and advance the ball.

---
[96] Isaiah 28:10, KJV

What exactly are those strategies?

One of the most vital is this: Speak the Word of God!

Stop parroting the negative stuff you're always hearing from the world and the devil, and say only what God says—about yourself, your family, your future, and your life.

God's Word is powerful. When we speak it and release our faith, it clears a path for His will to be done. It removes hindrances, straightens out twisted situations, and brings the promises of God to pass for us. It bulldozes demonic obstacles out of our way.

The prophet Isaiah described it like this:

> Listen! I hear the voice of someone shouting, "Make a highway for the LORD through the wilderness. Make a straight, smooth road through the desert for our God. Fill the valleys and level the hills. Straighten out the curves and smooth off the rough spots. Then the glory of the LORD will be revealed, and all people will see it together. The LORD has spoken!... Shout!" [97]

If you're wondering how our words could possibly make that much difference, read the first chapter of Genesis. You'll see that we live in a word-created, voice-activated system. God made everything in this universe by speaking. He said, "Let there be light!" and

---

[97] Isaiah 40:3-5

there was light. He said, "Let the dry land appear," and it did.

God's words still carry that same creative power today. As He says in Isaiah 55:10-11, "The rain and snow come down from the heavens and stay on the ground to water the earth. They cause the grain to grow, producing seed for the farmer and bread for the hungry. It is the same with my word. I send it out, and it always produces fruit. It will accomplish all I want it to, and it will prosper everywhere I send it."

The only difference between God's Word at creation and God's Word now is this: We're the ones speaking it. He has entrusted it to us and instructed us to declare it by faith over our lives. As His children, created in His image,

> Kings reign by speaking. They don't pick up shovels and do physical labor when they want something done. They give commands...and so should we.

we've been commissioned, in Christ Jesus, to reign as kings in life, by divine decree.

Think about that. Kings reign by speaking. They don't pick up shovels and do physical labor when they want something done. They give commands...and so should we. That's how we're supposed to exercise our spiritual authority. We're to go into speaking mode, use scripture, and say what God says about the situations that concern us. We're to use words to forbid evil things and bring forth good things.

Just as God did in the Book of Genesis, we can send out our words and they'll accomplish what we send them to do.

That's why Jesus said:

> Have faith in God. For verily I say unto you, That whosoever shall say unto this mountain, Be thou removed, and be thou cast into the sea; and shall not doubt in his heart, but shall believe that those things which he saith shall come to pass; he shall have whatsoever he saith (Mark 11:22-23, KJV).

IT STARTS WITH YOUR HEART

Think of words like the gear shift in a car. When we speak in agreement with God, our lives move forward. But when we speak contrary to His Word, we either sit idle (at best) or move backward.

Our words are always working, either for us or against us. So if we want to keep making progress, we'll have to be quiet sometimes. We must learn to zip our lips—especially when people mistreat us and our flesh gets riled up, because that's when we're most likely to throw our verbal gearshift in reverse.

> We must learn to zip our lips—especially when our flesh gets riled up, because that's when we're most likely to throw our verbal gearshift in reverse.

We can't talk out of both sides of our mouth and still expect our words to move mountains. We can't speak love and faith one minute and bitterness and spite the next, and enjoy the kind of power Jesus said we could have. The bad things we say will spoil the good, which is the reason James 3:9-13 gives us this warning:

> No one can tame the tongue. It is an uncontrollable evil, full of deadly poison. Sometimes it praises our Lord and Father, and sometimes it breaks out into curses against those who have been made in the image of God. And so blessing and cursing come pouring out of the same mouth. Surely, my brothers and sisters, this is not right! Does a spring of water bubble out with both fresh water and bitter water? Can you pick olives from a fig tree or figs from a grapevine? No, and you can't draw fresh water from a salty pool. If you are wise and understand God's ways, live a life of steady goodness so that only good deeds will pour forth.

I know what you may be thinking. *If no one can tame the tongue, how can I consistently speak the right words?*

You do it by starting with your heart.

Jesus said, "whatever is in your heart determines what you say."[98] So if you fill your heart with God's Word, you'll speak it almost without thinking. The

---
[98] Matthew 12:34

Word will flow out of you as naturally as milk flows out of a milk carton—because that's what's in you.

When you do happen to run into situations that leave you speechless, you'll be able to wait in silence for the guidance of the Holy Spirit because the Bible promises He "will give you the right words when the time comes."[99] That means, of course, you'll be a lot quieter at times than most people. But that's okay. It's good to be a person of few words. God makes that quite clear. He says:

- Don't talk too much, for it fosters sin. Be sensible and turn off the flow! (Proverbs 10:19).
- A truly wise person uses few words; a person with understanding is even-tempered (Proverbs 17:27).
- Do not be quick with your mouth, do not be hasty in your heart to utter anything before God. God is in heaven and you are on earth, so let your words be few. As a dream comes when there are many cares, so the speech of a fool when there are many words (Ecclesiastes 5:2-3).
- Dear friends, be quick to listen, slow to speak, and slow to get angry (James 1:19).
- Words from a wise man's mouth are gracious, but a fool is consumed by his own lips. At the beginning his words are folly; at the end they are wicked madness—and the fool multiplies words (Ecclesiastes 10:12-14).

---
[99] Luke 12:12, MSG

If you've always had a sharp, quick tongue, you might be groaning right now and wondering if there's any hope for you. But let me assure you, there is. You can start changing today if you'll begin to declare the Word over yourself in this area. Instead of saying, "I'm always getting mad and putting my foot in my mouth!" say, "I'm always quick to listen, slow to speak, and slow to get angry. My words are gracious. I'm sensible and use few words." Before long, you'll begin to notice a difference in your responses.

"But Vikki, I don't believe in that positive confession stuff."

Yes, you do. That's how you got born again. You acted on Romans 10:9 that says, "If thou shalt confess with thy mouth the Lord Jesus, and shalt believe in thine heart that God hath raised him from the dead, thou shalt be saved." The word *confess* in that verse is the Greek word *homologeo* which means *to say the same thing*. You said what God says about getting saved and it came to pass.

You can use that same principle in a broader sense by applying it to every aspect of salvation—including deliverance, protection, healing, and prosperity, and sanctification. By saying with your mouth what God says and believing it in your heart, you can receive everything He has provided. You can become all He has called you to be.

DOODLING IN THE DUST

If you want to see an example of how to use words to win spiritual victories, all you have to do is study Jesus. He did it non-stop. Without fail. Even in complicated, pressurized situations.

Like the one He faced with the woman caught in adultery.

The Pharisees showed up with her right in the middle of one of Jesus' teaching meetings. Shoving her in front of the crowd, they asked Him a question. "The law of Moses says to stone her. What do you say?"[100]

Just as in the other incidents we've studied, the Pharisees weren't looking for information from Jesus. They were trying to trap him into saying something they could use against Him—which is exactly what the devil does to us. He uses agitation, hurt, and mistreatment to pressure us into saying something unloving, something contrary to the Word. If we do, then he uses what we say against us. So we must train ourselves to stop and think before we open our mouth.

That's what Jesus did in this situation. He stooped down and silently doodled in the dust with His finger. Because His mission was to reveal the love of the Father while also upholding the Mosaic Law, His words had to be wisely chosen. So He refused to give in to the Pharisees demands for an immediate answer. He left them waiting for Him while He waited on God.

People often get sidetracked wondering what Jesus wrote in the dirt that day. But it doesn't really matter.

---

[100] John 8:5

What's important is the fact that He refused to let anyone pressure Him into speaking prematurely. He took all the time He needed to hear from God so that He would say the right thing. He taught us by example that silence is sometimes better than a quick answer.

Once He knew how to reply, He stood up and said, "The sinless one among you, go first: Throw the stone."[101] Then, uninterested in their response, He went right back to doodling in the dust.

It was the perfect reply, of course. There wasn't a person in the crowd who hadn't sinned. None of them was qualified to condemn the woman. So they crept away and Jesus was free to express the love of God by saying,

> Our words are so important. Like bullets fired from a gun, once they're spoken they can never be taken back.

"Woman, where are they? Does no one condemn you?"

"No one, Master."

"Neither do I," said Jesus. "Go on your way. From now on, don't sin."[102]

Our words are so important. Like bullets fired from a gun, once they're spoken they can never be taken back. That's why it's always better to be too slow than too quick to speak. When we're not sure what the Lord would have us say in a situation, waiting is always the right course. According to Proverbs 18:21: "What you say can

---

[101] v. 7, MSG
[102] vv. 10-11, MSG

mean life or death. Those who speak with care will be rewarded."[103] Your future depends on that critical moment between the infraction and your response. So choose in advance when things are calm what you're going to do. Decide ahead of time to keep your mouth shut in every situation until you can speak with wisdom and love.

In the end, you'll always be glad you did.

GET OUT THERE AND DO SOMETHING GOOD

Another offensive strategy you can use to score points against the devil is this: Get out there and do something good.

Don't just wait for him to attack and then try to counter him by suppressing your fleshly reactions. Be proactive. Purposely override your flesh with the fruit of the Spirit. Look for ways to be a blessing everywhere you go.

"For this is your calling—to do good and one day to inherit all the goodness of God."[104]

You'll be amazed how much easier it is to run roughshod over the devil and his temptations when you're focused on that calling. You won't have time to get offended. You'll be too busy obeying the Lord and pouring out His love to others.

Galatians 5:16-23 confirms that. It says:

> Walk in the Spirit, and you shall not fulfill the lust of the flesh. For the flesh lusts against

---

[103] The New Century Version
[104] 1 Peter 3:9, Phillips Translation

the Spirit, and the Spirit against the flesh; and these are contrary to one another, so that you do not do the things that you wish. But if you are led by the Spirit, you are not under the law [of the flesh]. Now the works of the flesh are evident...But the fruit of the Spirit is love, joy, peace, longsuffering, kindness, goodness, faithfulness, gentleness, self-control (NKJV).

As believers, we don't have to "work up" that fruit of the Spirit. It's already inside us. God put it there when we were born again. But we must practice yielding to it. We must develop it by seeking out opportunities every day to reach out to others with love, joy, peace, patience, kindness, and goodness. Then we can not only avoid the devil's traps ourselves, we can help others avoid them too.

My friend, Cathy Duplantis, does that all the time. She's always bringing God's goodness on the scene—and I've been the beneficiary of it more than once.

I'll never forget what she did for me one day back 1997. My first book, *Aim Your Child like an Arrow*, had just been published. I could hardly contain my excitement. So at the first opportunity, when I was at a meeting with a number of my friends, I gave a copy to one of them I highly respected. "This is my first book!" I said.

Anticipating her response, I waited for her to thumb through it or congratulate me.

But instead she tossed it aside without even looking at it.

My face must have revealed my shock because Cathy hastily intervened. "Can I have a copy?" she exclaimed. "Would you sign it for me?"

I knew Cathy wasn't interested in a book about raising children. Her daughter was already grown and married. But that didn't matter. She was on a mission to be a blessing. So she kindly reached out and restored the situation before it had a chance to hurt me. She overshadowed the indifference of my friend with her enthusiasm, and undermined the devil's plan.

That day, I was like a quarterback who'd thrown a pass only to have the receiver fumble the ball. Given the opportunity, the devil would have grabbed that ball and run with it. But Cathy refused to let him. Quick to respond in love, she recovered the fumble and scored the points that won the game. She not only salvaged that one play, she set an example for me I'll remember the rest of my life.

Cathy fulfilled her calling as a believer that day. She acted like Jesus "who went about doing good, and healing all that were oppressed of the devil."[105] Thank God, we can all follow that example. We can choose to recover and restore people instead of ignore them when they're hurt, insulted, or embarrassed.

But to do that we must pay attention to those around us instead of always being focused on ourselves.

---

[105] Acts 10:38, KJV

We must get aggressive about developing the qualities we need to live like winners.

God has already done His part. He's already put those qualities inside our born again spirit. "He has by His own action given us everything that is necessary for living the truly good life...."[106]

Now we must do our part.

As the Apostle Peter said:

> Do your utmost from your side and see that your faith carries with it real goodness of life. Your goodness must be accompanied by knowledge, your knowledge by self-control, your self-control by the ability to endure. Your endurance too must always be accompanied by devotion to God; that in turn must have in it the quality of brotherliness, and your brotherliness must lead on to Christian love. If you have these qualities existing and growing in you then it means that knowing our Lord Jesus Christ has not made your lives either complacent or unproductive. The man whose life fails to exhibit these qualities is short-sighted—he can no longer see the reason why he was cleansed from his former sins. Set your minds, then, on endorsing by your conduct the fact that God has called and chosen you. If you go along the lines I have indicated above, there is no reason why you should stumble...

---

[106] 2 Peter 1:3, Phillips Translation

All too often, we stumble instead of scoring because we take our eyes off the goal. We get "short-sighted." We lose track of the fact that the whole point of this game is to do good, to be a blessing to others, and express the love of Jesus everywhere we go.

That's what we're all about. It's the big picture. So let's say like Paul did, "This one thing I do, forgetting those things which are behind, and reaching forth unto those things which are before, I press toward the mark for the prize of the high calling of God in Christ Jesus."[107]

> Let's play some serious offense and win this game.

Let's play some serious offense and win this game.

---

[107] Philippians 3:13-14, KJV

10

THE DEVIL'S GREATEST FEAR

We are all one body, we have the same Spirit, and we have all been called to the same glorious future.
Ephesians 4:4

Do you want to know what makes the devil tremble?

Believers living in unity.

The very thought of it has terrified him for more than 2,000 years. Ever since he heard Jesus pray for His disciples in the Garden of Gethsemane:

> My prayer for all of them is that they will be one, just as you and I are one, Father, that just as you are in me and I am in you, so they will be in us, and the world will believe you sent me.[108]

---
[108] John 17:21

Even the devil could figure out that prayer was important. As the last earthly request Jesus made for His followers before He laid down His life for them, it carried great weight. And the thought of it coming to pass surely sent chills down Satan's spine.

He must have hoped against hope the prayer had been unrealistic. That Jesus had finally asked for the impossible by asking for His disciples to be unified.

I mean, really. Could even God bring such a fussy, touchy, competitive group of people into harmony with each other?

This was the same bunch that had argued behind Jesus' back about which one of them was the greatest! They'd failed miserably to get along with each other even while Jesus was physically present with them. How were they supposed to do any better after He was gone? How would they or any disciples in the future ever be able to live as one?

I suspect the devil repeatedly asked himself such questions for the first few weeks after Jesus' resurrection. Then, on the day of Pentecost, he got the answer. He saw 120 believers gathered together in the upper room praying "with one accord."[109]

Given what Jesus had said in Gethsemane, the devil knew it meant trouble for him. And what happened next confirmed it.

> Suddenly there came a sound from heaven, as of a rushing mighty wind, and it filled the

---
[109] Acts 1:14, NKJV

whole house where they were sitting. Then there appeared to them divided tongues, as of fire, and one sat upon each of them. And they were all filled with the Holy Spirit and began to speak with other tongues, as the Spirit gave them utterance (Acts 2:2-4).

In that historic instant, demons and believers alike saw what happens when Christians come together as one. They saw why Jesus' made unity His final earthly request:

Unity ushers in the supernatural.

It opens the door for the power of the Holy Spirit.

What happened on Pentecost left no doubt about it. While the devil watched with helpless horror, 120 supernaturally empowered, Holy Spirit anointed believers spilled out onto the streets of Jerusalem, testifying to the power of God in languages they'd never learned. Peter preached a sermon so fiery that 3,000 people got saved.

> Given what Jesus had said in Gethsemane, the devil knew it meant trouble for him. And what happened next confirmed it.

I think it's safe to assume Satan realized that day he would spend the rest of his time on earth fighting to keep believers from ever getting into that kind of unity again.

YOU CAN'T BE ANOINTED ALL BY YOURSELF

I know what you're probably thinking. *That was Pentecost! It was a unique moment in time. Unity among believers doesn't always produce such supernatural results.*

Yes it does. It may not always be accompanied by a spiritual storm of wind and fire, but it always releases the anointing of the Holy Spirit in our lives. Check out Psalm 133 and you'll see what I mean. It says:

> Behold, how good and how pleasant it is for brethren to dwell together in unity! It is like the precious ointment upon the head, that ran down upon the beard, even Aaron's beard: that went down to the skirts of his garments; As the dew of Hermon, and as the dew that descended upon the mountains of Zion: for there the LORD commanded the blessing, even life for evermore (vv. 1-3, KJV).

Notice the first thing that passage says about unity is it's *good* and *pleasant*. Wouldn't you say that in this day and hour, when there's so much trouble and upheaval on the earth, being able to enjoy a good and pleasant life requires supernatural power?

Certainly it does. And we can have that power if we'll live in peace, not only with God, but with the people around us. If we refuse to get into strife, we can walk in the blessing even when the rest of the world is staggering under the curse. Others may not choose to live in harmony with us, but if we'll commit to it on our side, we can enjoy what Psalm 133 calls "the precious ointment."

When something is precious, it's considered to be of great value, usually because it's rare or uncommon—and believers who live in unity are definitely rare. That's one reason why so few Christians experience the abundant life Jesus provided. It's not necessarily because they don't have faith. They truly believe abundant life belongs to them. They can quote scriptures like "He who is in you is greater than he who is in the world,"[110] and "In all these things we are more than conquerors through Him who loved us."[111] But those verses aren't a reality in their lives.

Pardon me for being blunt, but I want to ask you something. Are they a reality in yours? Are you really living as more than a conqueror every day and overcoming every attack of the devil?

If you're not, I have some sobering news: There's a reason for it. "The curse causeless shall not come."[112]

If you're not enjoying the good life the Bible describes, you're missing it somewhere. And it's possibly in the area of unity because that's where God

---
[110] 1 John 4:4
[111] Romans 8:37, NKJV
[112] Proverbs 26:2, KJV

commands the blessing. That's where the precious ointment flows.

The ointment (or anointing oil) was an Old Testament symbol of the anointing of the Holy Spirit. It represented the saving, healing, delivering, victory-producing power of God. When a high priest, like Aaron, was set into office, the ointment was poured over his head. From there it flowed onto his beard and his priestly garments.

As Psalm 133 specifically points out, the oil didn't leap, airborne, from the priest's head to his feet. It didn't skip from his beard to his big toe. It traveled from his head, to his neck, to his shoulders, to his chest, and so forth, until his whole body was drenched.

Why is that important?

Because it reveals a crucial New Testament reality. It shows how the anointing flows today from Jesus, who is the Head and High Priest of the Church, to us as believers. It reminds us that we can't be anointed all by ourselves.

> We can't operate like spiritual lone rangers and say to Jesus, "It's just you and me, Lord!" and then ignore everybody else.

We can't operate like spiritual lone rangers and say to Jesus, "It's just you and me, Lord!" and then ignore everybody else. We have to connect with the other Christians because the anointing we need to fulfill our destiny flows to us not only from Jesus but through each another.

That's the reason the Church is called "the Body of Christ." As believers, we really do function like a spiritual version of a physical body. In Jesus, we're "joined and knit together by what every joint supplies." We're built up and made complete by "the effective working by which every part does its share."[113]

We have to be in harmony with other believers to get our full spiritual supply. So if we're disjointed from each other, we're going to fall short of God's plan for our lives.

Think for a moment about how your physical body works. If you're sitting on the beach and you want to wiggle your toes in the sand, your brain can't just bypass the rest of your body and communicate directly with your toes to tell them what to do. The signals from your brain must travel all the way through your body to get to your toes. Your feet have to get involved. Your legs have to get involved. It's a joint operation.

The same is true spiritually. Just as "the human body has many parts, but the many parts make up only one body, so it is with the body of Christ…The eye can never say to the hand, 'I don't need you.' The head can't say to the feet, 'I don't need you.'"[114]

The idea of natural body parts saying they don't need each other may sound silly, but in the Church we see it all the time. We see believers God created to be "fingers" in the Body of Christ trying to do their job

---

[113] Ephesians 5:16, NKJV
[114] 1 Corinthians 12:12, 20-21

all by themselves, acting like they don't need any help from other parts of the Body.

Sometimes they even get angry at the other parts. They look at the elbow and decide they don't like it because it's different than them. It bends weird. It's crusty and ugly. It's all wrinkly. "I'm not like the elbow," they say. "I'm more attractive and more useful. I can dial telephone numbers, scratch itches, signal waiters, and push elevator buttons. All the elbow can do is bend. I don't really need it."

That kind of attitude is common among believers. And it's a major problem. It keeps us from completing the assignments Jesus gives us. When we ignore or get in strife with each other, we don't have what it takes to do our job. Our spiritual supply is cut off. Things stop working right in our life. We start to feel like we're missing something—and so do those around us.

Look again at Ephesians 4:16, this time in *New Living Translation*. It says, "Under his [Christ's] direction, the whole body is fitted together perfectly. As each part does its own special work, it helps the other parts grow, so that the whole body is healthy and growing and full of love."

The revelation that we each do "our own special work" is vital because that's where we often get tripped up. We want everybody else to be like we are, think like we think, and do what we do. But that's not how it's supposed to be. Jesus didn't make us all to be the same. That would be boring for Him. He enjoys variety. So

He made each one of us unique and gave us our own special work to do.

Dennis and I were sharply reminded of that fact many years ago at a minister's meeting. As Bible teachers, we were taken aback when a well-respected preacher said, "If you're not planting churches, you're not doing anything for God!" His attitude could have derailed our destiny if we'd taken it to heart because we're not called to plant churches. We're called to travel and minister the Word to believers.

Another time, a successful Christian businessman said to Dennis, "The Lord already has enough preachers. What He needs is more businessmen to finance the Gospel. You should go into business." The man was trying to offer good, fatherly advice, but he was completely wrong. Jesus didn't create Dennis to do what that man did. If he stopped preaching and became a businessman, he would totally miss out on God's plan!

On yet another occasion, a pastor and friend of ours pulled us aside and asked, "When are you going to listen to God and start pastoring?" The question all but invalidated our ministry. "How much time have you spent praying about our calling?" I asked him. Although he didn't respond, I knew the answer: *None.*

I'm not criticizing those people. They meant well. They just made the mistake of thinking everybody in the Body of Christ should be like them.

We all make that mistake at times. We all say things like, "If I were the pastor of this church, I'd do this or that. If I were in charge of the women's ministry or the youth ministry, I'd make some changes." But it's time we stopped that kind of talk. It's time we focused on our own job and quit thinking other people are wrong just because they're different from us.

Different isn't wrong, it's just...*different!*

Instead of complaining about it, we should enjoy it. The finger Christians should look at the elbow Christians and say, "Wow, they're cool! They're interesting. They're nothing like I am. I need them!"

> It's time we focused on our own job and quit thinking other people are wrong just because they're different from us.

"But Vikki," you might say, "some people just annoy me! Like the woman who sits behind me in church every Sunday. She wears black fingernail polish and has a tattoo. I don't agree with that."

Too bad. We don't get to pick and choose between members of the Body. We're fitly joined together. There's something I need that has to come through you, and something you need that has to come through me. If we get crosswise with each other, it's like cutting off our own feet. We're wounded and incomplete. We're not going to get the full supply of the anointing Jesus wants us to have.

So if somebody else's differences start agitating you, just close your eyes. Don't look at what they're doing. Make up your mind that it doesn't matter what the elbow, or the shoulders, or the hips, or the feet of this Body look or act like. You're going to live at peace with them all. You're going to stay connected.

You give your supply, I'll give mine, and all of us can grow in love and be healthy.

THE WORLD WILL SIT UP AND TAKE NOTICE

Please understand, I'm not saying we all have to agree on everything. We don't all need to have the same doctrine, think the same thoughts, or wear the same kinds of clothes. That's not our aim. As Christians, we can disagree about all kinds of things and still have what the Bible calls "the unity of the faith."[115] That kind of unity centers on our common belief in God and in Jesus as Lord and Savior. It joins us together as members of the same spiritual family.

What would happen if we ditched all our petty disputes and really started acting like loving, unified Christian family?

Jesus told us through His prayer in John 17. He said:

> I am praying not only for these disciples but also for all who will ever believe in me because of their testimony. My prayer for all of them is that they will be one, just as you and I are one, Father—that just as you are in me and I am in you, so they will be in us, and the world will believe you sent me. I have given them the glory you gave me, so that they may be one, as we are—I in them and you in me, all being

[115] Ephesians 4:13, NKJV

perfected into one. Then the world will know that you sent me and will understand that you love them as much as you love me (John 17:20-23).

According to Jesus, our persuasive preaching and clever evangelistic strategies aren't the only thing that will convince the world of the truth of the Gospel. What will win people is our unity, our love for each other, and the absence of strife in the Church.

No wonder the world hasn't yet been swept into God's Kingdom. No wonder the heathen haven't been banging down the church doors begging to get saved. They haven't yet seen us living together in harmony, refusing to get upset with each other. They haven't yet seen the anointing flowing unhindered in us, around us, and through us, saturating us like the oil saturated Aaron in Psalm 133, from head to foot.

When that happens the world will sit up take notice. Unsaved people will look at us and say, "There's something different about you. You're peaceful. You love each other. You don't fight and backbite and gossip. You live good and pleasant lives. You're blessed!"

Don't you want people to be talking like that about the Church?

I do too.

But what's more important, Jesus wants it. So that's what we should be striving toward. Above all else, we should be "endeavoring to keep the unity of the Spirit in the bond of peace."[116] We should be setting our focus on the Lord, on becoming one with Him—in thought, word, and deed—because as we become one with Him, we'll become one with each other.

Of course, that will require more than a half-hearted effort. We can't just nonchalantly say, "Yeah, I'd like to be more like Jesus. Whatever." We have to make a serious commitment. The kind that keeps us asking all the time, *How would Jesus respond in this situation? What does He think about this? Does my attitude about it line up with His? Is it pleasing to Him?*

If we would focus that intensely on pleasing the Lord, we wouldn't even notice a lot of stuff that would otherwise agitate us. Because our eyes would be on Him, we wouldn't even see the offensive behavior of others. By contrast, if we focus on ourselves, we see every little thing that's wrong with the people around us. We see where everybody is falling short. We start thinking about what they should do and shouldn't do. And before long, we're in strife with somebody.

Ask me how I know.

You guessed it: From lots of experience.

That's why I like to keep this passage from Colossians in the forefront of my mind:

> Since you have been raised to new life with Christ, set your sights on the realities of heaven, where Christ sits at God's right hand in the place of honor and power. Let heaven fill

---
[116] Ephesians 4:3, NKJV

your thoughts. Do not think only about things down here on earth. For you died when Christ died, and your real life is hidden with Christ in God (Colossians 3:1-3).

Life can be really great when we operate like our real lives are hidden with Christ in God. Nothing anybody says or does can touch us. Other people can't pull us off course or strip us of the anointing by getting us into strife because we're not focused on them. Our sights are set on Jesus and becoming one with Him.

I learned one time when Dennis and I were preparing to go deer hunting just how important setting your sights can be. We'd gone to the rifle range so that I could fire some test shots with a rifle I'd recently been given. I took aim at the target that was about 100 yards away and pulled the trigger. But I didn't hit the bull's-eye. Instead, all my shots went through just above it to the left.

"I missed!" I said in disgust.

"That's why we're here," Dennis replied. "We're going to set the sights on your rifle." After looking through the scope at the hole I'd made in the target, he made an adjustment. "Try again," he said.

The next time the shots were closer to the mark but still off. Dennis made another adjustment and the next time I put all the shots through the bull's-eye.

I may not be Annie Oakley, but I'm smart enough to know this: I never would have hit that bull's-eye if

I'd just kept shooting at it, hoping for a better result. I had to set my sights on my rifle.

The same is true in our Christian life. We get what we set our sights on. Our problem has been that we've been setting our sights too low, on the things of the earth, on ourselves, and everybody else.

But we could be setting our sights on heaven. (I don't mean just looking forward to going there someday in the sweet by and by. I mean focusing on what heaven has to offer us right here and now.) We could be saying, "Lord, I love You! I want the world to see You through me. I want to be compassionate and good. I want to reveal Your mercy to the world. You've freely given me so much love and favor, I want to freely give it to others. I want to be a living letter from You for everybody to read!"

> Our problem has been that we've been setting our sights too low, on the things of the earth, on ourselves, and everybody else.

If we'll raise our sights and live to reveal Jesus, we'll be able to hit the mark of unity in Psalm 133. And that's where the Lord has commanded the blessing. That's where His supernatural power always flows.

11

UNSTOPPABLE POWER... OR EASY PREY?

> *Be careful! Watch out for attacks from the Devil, your great enemy. He prowls around like a roaring lion, looking for some victim to devour.*
> 1 Peter 5:8

The Bible tells us again and again that miraculous things happen when people of faith work together in harmony. Take what the Book of Ecclesiastes says, for example. "Two can accomplish more than twice as much as one, for the results can be much better."[117] Logically, that doesn't compute. You'd think that two people would be able to accomplish exactly twice as much as one. But that's not what the verse says.

It says they can accomplish more.

How much more?

---
[117] Ecclesiastes 4:9, TLB

The scripture sets no limit. It indicates that when we're in unity, we're unlimited because we can tap into the limitless power of the anointing.

In Matthew 18:19, Jesus said it like this. "If two of you agree on earth concerning anything that they ask, it will be done for them by My Father in heaven."[118]

His statement raises a question: If two can receive anything they ask when they're in agreement, what could 60 believers accomplish by sticking together, refusing to allow the devil any access to their church and community?

Leviticus 26:8 gives us the answer. It says, "Five of you will chase a hundred, and a hundred of you will chase ten thousand! All your enemies will fall beneath the blows of your weapons."

The power of unity and agreement releases supernatural multiplication. While five of us in agreement can defeat 100 problems, remove 100 burdens, put 100 demons out of business, 100 of us working together can whip 10,000. Do the math, you'll see that's a hundred-fold increase.

Have you ever wanted to receive a hundred-fold return on your giving? Have you ever wished you could bring revival to your city? This is the way to do it. Walk in unity, harmony, and agreement with other believers.

When we operate together in unity, as one Body, we can't be stopped!

The devil knows that, so he's always working to keep us in strife. He's perpetually trying to counteract

---

[118] NKJV

the power of unity by activating its reciprocal: "Every kingdom divided against itself is brought to desolation, and every city or house divided against itself will not stand."[119]

If you've ever watched one of those television documentaries about lions in Africa, you know how deadly division can be. Lions depend on it. They don't just gallop into the middle of a herd of wildebeests and attack. They creep around in the grass, staying low so they won't be seen, and wait for one of their victims to get isolated. They bide their time until a sick one starts to lag behind, or a curious one wanders into an isolated pasture because the grass looks greener there.

> If you've ever watched one of those television documentaries about lions in Africa, you know how deadly division can be. Lions depend on it.

Once the prey is alone, the lion lunges.

The rest of the wildebeest herd escapes, but the lone ranger of the herd, gets eaten.

The Bible says, "Be careful! Watch out for attacks from the Devil, your great enemy. He prowls around like a roaring lion, looking for some victim to devour."[120] Unlike the lions on the Discovery Channel, however, the devil doesn't only wait for Christians to wander off by themselves. He actively works to separate them

---
[119] Matthew 12:25
[120] 1 Peter 5:8

from each other. If he succeeds, they become his feasting ground.

Believers living in isolation are easy prey.

You might want to take that into account next time you're tempted to get cross with the people at your church. Before you decide to pull away from them and go it on your own for a while, think of the wildebeest.

Remind yourself that unity is protection.

USE THE WATER HOSE OF HARMONY TO PUT OUT THE FIRE

Here's another way unity can save your life. When a situation gets heated, pouring unity on it will cool things down. It will put out the fire when tempers start to flare.

It's amazing how well it works. Two people can be steaming with anger. They both can be furiously demanding their rights. But if just one of them will remember how precious unity is and remind themselves there's something bigger at stake, they can preserve the peace. They can prove that what Psalm 133:3 says is true. "Harmony is as refreshing as the dew from Mount Hermon that falls on the mountains of Zion."

Just look at what happened with Abraham and Lot. They were members of the same family but there was a time when things between their two households threatened to get ugly. Their flocks had multiplied until there wasn't enough pastureland to feed them all. Arguments were breaking out between their herdsmen.

Abraham had every right to settle the dispute by kicking his nephew off his land. He could have easily said, "Lot, take your flocks and your hateful herdsmen and get out!" After all, God had promised that land to Abraham. What's more, it was God's blessing on Abraham that had caused Lot's flocks to prosper.

But because he treasured unity, Abraham took a kinder approach to the problem. He said to Lot, "This arguing between our herdsmen has got to stop...After all, we are close relatives! I'll tell you what we'll do. Take your choice of any section of the land you want, and we will separate. If you want that area over there, then I'll stay here. If you want to stay in this area, then I'll move on to another place."[121]

Lot, the less spiritual of the two, chose the most fertile part of the land for himself. He took the well-watered, green valley and gave the arid land of Canaan to Abraham. His choice was selfish and unjust. But Abraham didn't complain about it. He didn't point out that Lot had benefitted from their relationship for years. He didn't rebuke Lot for taking advantage of his kindness and failing to reciprocate.

On the contrary, Abraham willingly gave up his "rights" in order to preserve their unity. Convinced that as long as he kept the peace God would bless him wherever he went, he deferred to Lot and happily moved to a more barren land...where God made him one of the richest men in the Bible.

---

[121] Genesis 13:8-9

Wasn't that a cool and refreshing solution? Don't you think we would all be more blessed if we acted like that?

Think how sweet the atmosphere of the Church could be if we were always more interested in giving to others rather than taking for ourselves. Think what would happen if we were always saying, "Here, you take the best. I insist! Don't be concerned about me, God will bless me richly. I'll be fine. I just want to be a blessing to you."

Wow. That would be heaven on earth, wouldn't it?

And we can have it if we'll dare to walk in unity.

MAKE ALLOWANCES FOR OTHER PEOPLE'S FAULTS

One way to promote that kind of unity is by following the simple instructions in Ephesians 4:2: "Be humble and gentle. Be patient with each other, making allowance for each other's faults because of your love."[122]

If you want to see how to make allowances for another person's faults, watch how mothers make excuses for their babies. If the baby gets fussy and irritable, the mother says, "Bless his heart! He must be

---
[122] TLB

hungry." Or "He must need a diaper change." If her toddler throws a tantrum, the mom says, "He must be sleepy. He must be teething."

Everybody else may be looking at the child thinking, *Get a clue, mom! Your kid is a brat.* But she just keeps making excuses for him.

Why can't we, as believers, do that for each other? If somebody gets cranky with us, why do we instantly get cranky with them in return? Why can't we make allowances for them because we love them? Give them the benefit of the doubt. Assume they've had an especially hard day and that we'd act the same way if we were in their shoes.

> If you want to see how to make allowances for another person's faults, watch how mothers make excuses for their babies.

It's often true, you know. People frequently are dealing with more than we realize. Maybe they had a fender bender on the way to work. Maybe their grandmother died yesterday. Maybe their kids have been sick. Any number of things could be behind their irritable behavior. But we don't usually take that into account. Instead we respond like they're out to get us, like they woke up this morning plotting to make us mad.

Let's break out of that pattern. Let's make allowances for people because we love them. Let's become those who plant seeds of peace and, in return, reap a harvest of goodness.[123]

We're believers. We can do this! We're born of God. "He has given us the Holy Spirit to fill our hearts with his love."[124] He has made us partakers of His own loving nature. All we have to do is yield to that nature on the inside of us and let it come out.

"But sometimes I just don't feel like it," you might say.

It doesn't matter. If we want to walk in the blessing of God, this isn't optional. It's mandatory. Jesus said, "I am giving you a new commandment: Love each other. Just as I have loved you, you should love each other."[125]

Notice, He didn't say, "I am giving you a new suggestion." He described love as a commandment. First John 4:21 uses the same word. It says, "God himself has *commanded* that we must love not only him but our Christian brothers and sisters, too."

The Apostle Paul said it this way:

> Since God chose you to be the holy people whom he loves, you must clothe yourselves with tenderhearted mercy, kindness, humility, gentleness, and patience. You must make allowance for each other's faults and forgive the person who offends you. Remember, the Lord forgave you, so you must forgive others. And the most important piece of clothing you must wear is love. Love is what binds us all together

---

[123] James 3:18
[124] Romans 5:5
[125] John 13:34

in perfect harmony. And let the peace that comes from Christ rule in your hearts. For as members of one body you are all called to live in peace (Colossians 3:12-15).

Notice that passage says if we're going to walk in love toward one another, one of the qualities we must exercise is patience. In the *King James Version* of the Bible it's called longsuffering.

Think of a bomb with a very long fuse. When the fuse is lit, it takes such a long time to burn that it's easy to put out the fire before the bomb explodes. That's a good picture of longsuffering.

Sadly, however, it's not a good picture of most Christians. Many of us tend to have a microscopically short fuse. All it takes is just a little spark, somebody saying the wrong thing or looking at us wrong, and—*ka-boom!*—we go off. How do we change that? We keep practicing patience. We bite our tongue and tell ourselves, "This irritation is nothing but the devil's yeast! I'm not going to get upset about it. I'm going to stay peaceful and free of strife." As we do that, our fuse will grow. It will take longer and longer for annoyances to get to us.

> All it takes is just a little spark, somebody saying the wrong thing or looking at us wrong, and—*ka-boom!*—we go off.

Having been kind of a rebel in former years, when the devil tries to exhaust my patience, I'll challenge him. I'll say, "Let's just see who can last the longest in this situation. I guarantee you, Devil, you're not going to wear me out. Someone is going down, and it's not me!"

Of course, I haven't always had that attitude. I was anything *but* loving and patient before I gave my life to Jesus. Having grown up in a rough, abusive home, I wasn't raised to be kind and sweet. I had to be tough just to survive.

After I was born again, though, I wanted my new nature to over-ride my old habits. I wanted love to control my life. So I started studying scriptures about it. I especially focused on First Corinthians 13. I looked up the definitions, synonyms, and antonyms of some of the words in that chapter so I could get a really clear picture of what it was saying. Then I put together a faith confession.

I declared over myself things like this:

God is love, and because I am born of God, I am born of love. Love defines me. Love in me is patient. I exhibit calm endurance even in difficulty. Love in me is kind. I'm friendly. I'm generous. I'm warm hearted, and I have an agreeable nature. Love in me is not envious or jealous. I'm content. I'm satisfied. I'm fulfilled and happy.

Love in me never boasts or is proud. I'm humble, unpretentious, discreet, meek, gentle, and modest. Love in me is not unbecoming. I act properly, decently, tactfully, and desirably. Love in me is not self-seeking. I seek the best in everyone. I always look for a way to bless others. Love in me is not touchy. Instead, I'm easy going, complimentary, safe, cheerful, good humored, pleasant, good, natured, predictable, and peaceful.

Love in me is not fretful. Instead, I'm at ease, calm, cool, relaxed, unworried, and unconcerned. Love in me is not resentful. I never hold a grudge. I'm forgiving, forbearing, exonerating. I make allowance for others and freely pardon and release them. My hopes are fadeless and I endure without weakening. Love in me never fails. I overcome this world by love.

I've declared those things over myself for years. Because I've kept them in front of my eyes, in my mouth, and in my ears, they've taken root in my heart and they're producing a harvest. The attributes of love have grown in me. These days, people can poke, poke, poke at me...and I won't explode.

DON'T JUST SUPPRESS IT, GET RID OF IT

It's only fair to warn you, this process also works in reverse. "Whatever you choose to obey becomes your master."[126] So, just as yielding to patience will lengthen your fuse, yielding to anger will shorten it. Just as ruling the passions of your flesh will make you spiritually stronger, failing to do so will make you

[126] Romans 6:6

increasingly weaker, powerless, and vulnerable to the devil's strategies.

As Proverbs 25:28 says, "If you cannot control your anger, you are as helpless as a city without walls, open to attack."

> Ruling the passions of your flesh will make you spiritually stronger, failing to do so will make you increasingly weaker, powerless, and vulnerable to the devil's strategies.

Too many Christians today have put themselves in that situation. They've torn down their spiritual wall of protection. They've sabotaged the answers to their prayers and made themselves easy targets for the devil. Disqualifying themselves for Christian service, they've become useless and unfruitful in the Kingdom of God, all because they've ignored verses like these:

- He who is slow to anger is better than the mighty, and he who rules his spirit than he who takes a city (Proverbs 16:32, KJV).
- A fool vents all his feelings, but a wise man holds them back (Proverbs 29:11).
- An angry man stirs up strife, and a furious man abounds in transgression (Proverbs 29:22).
- Don't sin by letting anger gain control over you. Think about it overnight and remain silent (Psalm 4:4).

- Let all bitterness and indignation and wrath (passion, rage, bad temper) and resentment (anger, animosity) and quarreling (brawling, clamor, contentions) and slander (evil-speaking, abusive or blasphemous language) be banished from you, with all malice (spite, ill will, or baseness of any kind). And become useful... (Ephesians 4:31-32, AMP).
- Now is the time to get rid of anger, rage, malicious behavior, slander, and dirty language (Colossians 3:8).

Look again at that last verse. It doesn't tell us to suppress anger; it says get rid of it. That might sound impossible to do if you have a history of what the world refers to as "anger management issues." But it can be done by following these scriptural steps.

First, acknowledge that you've given anger a foothold in your life. Confess it as sin and, obeying the instructions in First John 1:9, receive God's forgiveness and cleansing. Once you've been cleansed, you don't need to feel guilty anymore about the angry outbursts of the past. You can start over again with a clean slate.

Second, make an unwavering decision that you'll never again allow anger to control you.

Third, speak faith-filled words directly to the anger itself and the spirit behind it. Remind the devil that you are the temple of the Holy Spirit and anger has no right to remain in your life. Then, believing that "Whatever you forbid upon earth will be forbidden in heaven,"[127] command anger to leave you and forbid it to dominate you anymore. Any time anger tries to rise up and control you again, resist the devil and he will flee from you.[128]

I'm not going to claim it's a cakewalk. It's not. Especially when you're just starting to build your spiritual muscle of self-control, you'll be sorely tempted to blow your stack sometimes. In certain circumstances, you'll even feel justified. Somebody will say or do something to you that's so wrong, you'll think, *I have a right to get mad about this!*

> Once you've been cleansed, you don't need to feel guilty anymore about the angry outbursts of the past. You can start over again with a clean slate.

Whenever I have that thought, I remember what Colossians 3:11 says:

"Christ is all that matters."

What made me angry doesn't matter. My rights don't matter. How my flesh wants to respond doesn't matter. What matters is being like Jesus. What matters is living in the anointing, staying in the blessing, and stopping the devil from stealing my destiny.

Another passage that helps me when my fuse gets short and I feel like I want to explode is Matthew 7:13-14 in the Ben Campbell Johnson paraphrase. It

---

[127] Matthew 18:18, Phillips
[128] James 4:7

says that choosing God's way and living in the spirit, instead of the flesh, *requires focusing on your life and bringing it under control, but few choose to do it.*

I want to be one of the few, don't you? I want to be among God's most highly trained, elite forces. In other words, I want to be a spiritual member of God's SEAL Team 6.

Some people might consider that an odd thing to say, but I'm naturally patriotic and I've always appreciated the sacrifices made by the men and women in our nation's armed forces. Their heroic exploits inspire me. I especially admire special ops like SEALs, Delta, Green Beret, and Rangers. The almost unbearable training they endure to qualify for their dangerous mission makes them some of the most honorable people on earth in my eyes.

> I want to be among God's most highly trained, elite forces. In other words, I want to be a spiritual member of God's SEAL Team 6.

Long before the Navy's SEAL Team 6 became famous for killing Osama bin Laden, I enjoyed reading books about them. What impressed me most was the part of their training known as "hell week." During that week, the class usually shrinks by 90 percent. The only soldiers left at the end are those who can control their bodies and emotions even under the most stressful circumstances.

One SEAL Team sniper I read about could purposely slow his heart rate in order to fire his weapon between heartbeats. Now *that's* self control! Most of us can't even feel our heartbeat, but for a sniper aiming at a target 850 yards away, it can make the difference between a hit and a miss.

The way I see it, if natural soldiers can do things like that, then we as believers can exercise greater self-control than we realize. We can choose, in the moment someone strikes out against us, to restrain our anger and respond in love.

As one soldier said in the movie *Act of Valor*, "Put your pain in a box. Lock it down. No man is stronger than one who can harness his emotions."

It takes strength to live in harmony with other believers. Training to do it is tough, no question about it. But the reward is worth it, for there—in the place where brethren dwell together in unity—the LORD has pronounced his blessing, even life forevermore.[129]

---

[129] Psalm 133:3

12

THE PLACE WHERE DESTINIES GO TO DIE

> *O LORD of hosts, my King and my God. Happy are those who live in your house, ever singing your praise. Selah. Happy are those whose strength is in you, in whose heart are the highways to Zion. As they go through the valley of Baca they make it a place of springs; the early rain also covers it with pools. They go from strength to strength.*
> Psalm 84:3-7, NRSV

By now you've figured this out. It's better to stay out of the devil's trap of offense altogether than to get ensnared in it and then have to find a way out. It's better to refuse his bait at the outset than to swallow it—hook, line, and sinker—and then have to cough it back up.

The primary purpose of this book is to help you choose that better alternative. To help you avoid falling prey to the agitations around you. To equip you with the wisdom you need to remain composed and compassionate in the face of every kind of mistreatment so that you can live perpetually free from the yeast of offense.

Is such a life really possible?

Yes, it is.

Although none of us can avoid experiencing some hurts and betrayals, we can learn to respond to them in a way that prevents them from destroying, damaging, or even delaying our destiny. We can be like the believers in Psalm 84 who went through the Valley of Baca and just kept on moving.

In Old Testament times, the Valley of Baca was one shockingly offensive place. Literally called the Valley of Weeping, it was where human sacrifices were made to the demon god, Molech. It represented the worst kind of mistreatment and abuse.

No God-honoring Israelite ever wanted to go there. But from time to time it was unavoidable. They had to pass through it. When they did, they made it a point not to stop there. They understood, as we should, that the smartest thing to do when life's journey takes you through Baca is to step on the spiritual accelerator. Keep walking in love and faith. Keep trusting God to make everything work out for your good. Turn Baca into a place of blessing and emerge from it not only victorious but stronger than ever before.

Sadly, that's not always what we as New Testament believers do.

We often stumble and fall in our Valleys of Weeping. And instead of getting back up, we pitch a tent and camp out there for a while.

I've even known Christians who stayed stranded in Baca for years. Having tripped over some particularly grievous wrong that was dealt to them by their family, friends, or fellow believers, they allowed unforgiveness to completely stop them from moving forward. Rather than going *through* their valley of pain, they put down roots of bitterness there, settled in, and made it their home.

That's a very bad idea. In fact, it's downright dangerous because the place of bitterness is a place where prayers don't get answered. It's a place where the blessings and forgiveness of God can't reach us. It's a place where destinies go to die.

> We often stumble and fall in our Valleys of Weeping. And instead of getting back up, we pitch a tent and camp out there for a while.

Which is why Jesus warned us repeatedly to stay out of it.

"If you have anything against anyone," He said, "forgive him, that your Father in heaven may also forgive you your trespasses. But if you do not forgive, neither will your Father in heaven forgive your trespasses."[130]

---

[130] Mark 11:25-26, NKJV

Since we all need God's forgiveness (a lot!) you'd think we'd be eager to heed that counsel. You'd think we'd be willing to forgive anybody for anything, anytime, anywhere, just to keep the forgiveness pipeline open. It doesn't take a spiritual rocket scientist to see the wisdom in the old adage: Sow mercy. You're going to need it.

Yet when we've been hurt in a significant way—perhaps not just once but repeatedly—extending mercy and forgiveness to the people who hurt us can be tough to do. We can be tempted to look for a way around it. Lobbying for a little wiggle room, we might be inclined to ask Jesus, as Peter once did:

"Lord, how often should I forgive someone who sins against me? Seven times?"[131]

But the answer to that question is always the same. "I do not say to you, up to seven times, but up to seventy times seven."[132]

That's what Jesus told Peter. Then He drove the point home with a parable. It involved a king whose servant owed him millions of dollars. The servant was not able to pay so, according to Jesus:

> His master commanded that he be sold, with his wife and children and all that he had, and that payment be made. The servant therefore fell down before him, saying, 'Master, have patience with me, and I will pay you all.' Then the master of that servant was moved with

[131] Matthew 18:21
[132] v. 22, NKJV

compassion, released him, and forgave him the debt (vv. 25-27).

There's a phrase that's become popular in recent years. It's used to describe what happens when one person receives an undeserved gift or an act of kindness, and responds by doing the same for somebody else. It's called "Paying it forward."

Apparently, however, the servant in this parable had never heard of it. He went out and found a fellow servant who owed him only a few thousand dollars, and instead of paying forward the forgiveness that was extended to him, he did the opposite. He turned a deaf ear to the debtor's pleas and ordered him thrown into prison.

When the king heard about it, he was ticked. "'You wicked servant!' he said. 'I forgave you all that debt because you begged me. Should you not also have had compassion on your fellow servant, just as I had pity on you?'

"And his master was angry, and delivered him to the torturers until he should pay all that was due to him."[133]

That's a sobering story, isn't it?

But the most chilling part is what Jesus said at the end. "So My heavenly Father also will do to you if each of you, from his heart, does not forgive his brother his trespasses."[134]

---

[133] vv. 32-34, NKJV
[134] v. 35

Those words apply to us as Christians more than anyone else because, like the servant in the parable, we've been forgiven by God of a debt we could never repay. For us to receive that forgiveness and then refuse to extend it to others who owe us far less than we owed the Lord is unforgivable. If we do it, we'll be taken captive and kept in bondage by the kingdom of darkness.

We'll be turned over to the tormentors until we repent.

LOOK OUT! IT'S INFECTIOUS!

"But I just don't see why a little unforgiveness is such a big deal!" you might say. "After all, it doesn't affect anybody but me."

On the contrary, it can affect everyone you come in contact with. A form of devilish spiritual yeast, unforgiveness spreads.

"It takes only one wrong person among you to infect all the others..." wrote the Apostle Paul. "You know the saying, 'A bit of yeast makes the whole batch of dough rise.' You must remove the old yeast of sin so that you will be entirely pure. Then you will be like a new batch of dough without yeast...uncontaminated [as you are], for Christ."[135]

Notice Paul referred to yeast as a pollutant that contaminates our true identity. It causes us to act in a way that's contrary to who we really are.

---

[135] Galatians 5:9, 1 Corinthians 5:6-7, AMP

When we hold a grudge against someone, instead of behaving like born again children of God, we end up acting like modern day Pharisees. Looking down our noses all holier-than-thou, we pretend we've never needed mercy ourselves. But the truth is we've sinned and fallen short of God's standards just like the person we're condemning.[136]

Claiming to be Christians while being as judgmental and unforgiving as everybody else in the world is hypocritical. It contaminates our Christian witness. It agitates people who aren't saved.

Unbelievers get upset when we talk about going to church all the time and then we argue and fight like the devil. They want to see some real Christians. They're longing for us to reveal the nature of God by actually living what we profess to believe.

> Unbelievers get upset when we talk about going to church all the time and then we argue and fight like the devil. They want to see some real Christians.

Unbelievers aren't the only ones affected when we fail to forgive, either. Other Christians are too. When one believer yields to bitterness and starts judging other people, his attitude can spread through an entire congregation. It can practically tear a church apart.

---

[136] Romans 3:23 For all have sinned; all fall short of God's glorious standard.

No wonder Jesus said, "Beware of the yeast of the Pharisees—beware of their hypocrisy."[137] The hypocrisy of unforgiveness contaminates everybody—Christians and non-Christians alike.

Forgiveness, however, can reverse the damage. Just as the Kingdom of Darkness can expand its influence through the yeast of offense, we can expand the influence of God's Kingdom by choosing to be merciful. We can use the power of forgiveness to spread the light of God's love in our families, neighborhoods, workplaces, and churches.

As Jesus said, "the Kingdom of God…is like yeast used by a woman making bread, Even though she used a large amount of flour, the yeast permeated every part of the dough."[138]

Forgiveness is infectious!

Imagine how much good you could do if you made up your mind to become a carrier of it. Think what a positive effect it would have on the people around you if you said to yourself, *I'm getting rid of every bit of bitterness and judgment I've ever had against anybody. No matter what they've done to me, I'm going to extend mercy to them. I'm not going to criticize or say anything ugly about them. I'm going to speak only good, kind, edifying words to them and about them.*

I can tell you right now what will happen if you do that. People will notice the change in you. They'll be drawn to you. They may not say anything about it at

---

[137] Luke 12:1
[138] Luke 13:20-21

first, but after they watch you awhile and realize you're for real, they'll want what you have. They'll get hungry to know Jesus so that they become forgivers too.

YOU, LINDA RONDSTADT, AND ME

"But Vikki, you don't know how badly I've been hurt!" you might say. "I'm afraid if I forgive, I'll just be victimized again."

I understand how you feel. Like you, I can identify with the old song by Linda Ronstadt. *I've been cheated… been mistreated. I've been put down. I've been pushed round.* There's more than one reason that song hit the top of the charts. We've all had those experiences.

But unforgiveness won't protect us from them. It will only cause us additional hurt. It will eat us up on the inside, put the person who wronged us in control of our life, and prevent us from walking out our destiny.

Forgiveness, on the other hand, can give us our power back. Forgiving someone who's abused us enables us to look them in the eye and smile, knowing that we've broken their emotional and spiritual hold over us. They can't control us anymore because we have nothing against them.

I know what I'm talking about. When I was 16 years old, I suffered an emotional blow I thought I'd never get over. Just three weeks after my father died, my mother introduced me to her boyfriend—a married man she lived with for the next 30 years.

I was already angry about my father's death from cancer, but this man's unexpected presence in our home pushed me over the edge. As an unsaved, grieving teenager, I openly despised him and treated him as an intruder. Things in our home went from bad to worse as my hatred for him and my mother boiled over day after day.

After I became a Christian, the Holy Spirit began His transforming work in my life. He helped me gradually move beyond my anger. He opened my eyes to the guilt, shame, and misery my mother and her boyfriend suffered and gave me compassion for them.

Before this man died, the Lord gave me a vision. I saw both my hands extended in front of me, cupped together as though they were holding something. After a moment, the man's heart appeared in my hands. Then I heard the Lord's voice in my spirit. *"You have the power to crush his heart and allow him to continue suffering the guilt and shame of his sin. Or you can forgive him and release him from the prison of his lifelong bondage."*

> I can identify with the old song by Linda Ronstadt. *I've been cheated...been mistreated. I've been put down. I've been pushed round.*

In that moment, my perspective totally changed. I realized I was no longer a prisoner of my bitterness toward this man who had once caused me so much pain. Instead, he was the prisoner and I had the keys that would open his prison doors and set him free. I held in my hands the divine ability to release him from the guilt of his past, the shame of his hidden secrets, and his fear of being exposed and rejected.

The realization that I could possess such authority and power over another person's soul overwhelmed me. I knew it wasn't earthly power, the kind that inflates egos and feeds the flesh like fame, fortune, or influence might. It was the kind of power that comes from heaven. The kind Jesus spoke to His disciples about after His resurrection when He said, "If you forgive the sins of any, their sins have been forgiven them; if you retain the sins of any, they have been retained."[139] It was the power that Paul wrote to the Corinthian Christians about and said, "When you forgive this man [who has wronged you], I forgive him, too. And when I forgive him (for whatever is to be forgiven), I do so with Christ's authority."[140]

> In that moment, my perspective totally changed. I realized I was no longer a prisoner of my bitterness toward this man who had once caused me so much pain.

I'd always assumed such power belonged to God alone, but when I had that vision I understood as never before that He has given it to us, as believers, too.

The question was: What would I do with it?

Given the anguish this man had caused me and all the wrong he'd done, I could have chosen to let him

---
[139] John 20:22, NIV
[140] 2 Corinthians 2:10

suffer what he deserved. I could have let him die guilty and condemned. But as I considered that option, the truth of the Gospel pierced my heart: Jesus went to the cross to bear the punishment for my sins. Even though I didn't deserve to be forgiven, God had forgiven me nonetheless. How could I do anything less for this man than what had already been done for me?

The answer was obvious.

I couldn't.

So I utterly forgave him of the sins he'd committed against me and my family. I released him from every debt he owed us. When I did, supernatural power flowed—not only to him, but to me. As I liberated him from the torment of his sin, I was liberated myself.

Forgiveness always works that way. When we forgive those who have wronged us, the anointing of God described in Luke 4:18-19 goes to work both in the people we've forgiven and in us. It releases us from captivity and sets us free from oppression. It heals our wounded emotions and gives us access to Heaven's unlimited resources.

In the words of Psalm 84, forgiveness turns our Valley of Weeping into a place of blessing. It takes us from strength to strength.

It's ironic, really. Christians often cling to their bitterness because they're afraid they'll be weak and vulnerable without it. But the truth is just the opposite. Forgiveness is the ultimate manifestation of spiritual strength. We are never more powerful than when we forgive.

What's more, each time we forgive, we're further transformed into the image of Christ because He is forgiveness personified.

One man who understood that fact was Martin Luther King Jr. He experienced enough betrayal and injustice to make anyone bitter, but he chose to release every hurt and offense—again...and again...and again. "Forgiveness is not an occasional habit," he said. "It is a permanent attitude. We must develop and maintain the capacity to forgive. He who is devoid of the power to forgive is devoid of the power to love."

Another anonymous author said it this way:

> The language spoken in Heaven by the angels and the redeemed is the language of forgiveness. It will be the only language spoken there. No other language will be understood. It will be spoken by the seraphim and the cherubim and the whole angelic host as they praise God, the Author of forgiveness and of eternal salvation. It will be spoken by all the redeemed as they greet one another on the banks of the River of Life and gather around the throne of the Lamb and sing their song unto Him who loved them and washed them from the sins. But no one can learn that language after he gets to heaven. It must be learned here upon earth—in this world, and in this life.

Calling forgiveness "the language of Heaven" makes perfect sense to me. After all, Heaven is where forgiveness originated. Before mankind even existed, before God ever created us, He knew that we would sin; so in His great love, He designed a failsafe plan to save us. He put together the Plan of Redemption and foreordained the sacrifice of Jesus so that His forgiveness and blessings could be received by whosoever will.

> The language spoken in Heaven by the angels and the redeemed is the language of forgiveness. It will be the only language spoken there. No other language will be understood.

KEEP GOING BACK UNTIL YOU GET ALL THE GRACE YOU NEED

If you've suffered serious mistreatment or abuse at some point in your past, you may think I'm oversimplifying this issue. You may feel like I'm insensitive to your pain. But I assure you, I'm not. Neither is Jesus. He cares deeply about your wounded soul and He is committed to healing and restoring your damaged emotions.

He also understands that can take time.

I once talked with a woman whose husband struggled with severe depression. He'd suffered from it ever since, as a child, he'd witnessed the brutal murder of his parents and sibling. The night they were killed, as he was lying in the hospital recovering from his own physical wound, a group of elders from his church came to visit him.

Their mission?

To tell this young, heartbroken orphan that he must immediately forgive his parents' killer. God required it, they said.

Those elders—well-meaning as they might have been—made a grave mistake. They gave that little boy no time to process what had happened. No time to receive from God the grace and comfort he needed to deal with his tragic loss. Instead, riding roughshod over his anguished heart, they pushed him into a legalistic form of forgiveness that has left him emotionally crippled ever since.

Jesus doesn't do that kind of thing. He doesn't ignore our pain. He doesn't push us to do what we're not emotionally or spiritually prepared to do. Always patient and kind toward us, He says:

> Come into fellowship with me if you are tired and burdened, and I will refresh and release you. Take the burden of responsibility I give you and thereby discover your life and your destiny. I am gentle and humble; I am willing to relate to you and to permit you to learn at your own rate; then, in fellowship with me you will discover the meaning of your life. My fellowship will release you, and my companionship will direct you on your journey (Matthew 11:28-30, Ben Campbell Johnson Paraphrase).

Jesus is good. He'll walk you through the process of forgiveness with tenderness and compassion. He'll let you move through it at your own rate, even if it takes a while.

I can testify to it. There have been times when I said to Him, "Lord, I realize I have to forgive this person, and by faith I am. But right now, I'm just hurt!" In response, He always gave me the emotional space I needed. He always let me know that if I wasn't there yet, He'd wait. He'd keep working with me as long as I would keep working with Him. And, eventually, together we'd get the job done.

Exactly how do you go about working with Jesus on the issue of forgiveness?

You draw near to Him through prayer and the Word. You ask Him to help you fully pardon the people who've hurt you. You act on Hebrews 4:16 which says, "Let us therefore draw near with confidence to the throne of grace, that we may receive mercy and may find grace to help in time of need."[141]

Grace is God's supernatural ability that empowers us to do what we cannot do on our own. And He can give us more than enough of it to overcome any and all hurts, offenses, and betrayals. Sometimes, though, we can't receive all we need with just one prayer. Especially if we have a lot of emotional pain, we may have to go back to the Lord to ask for help again and again. We may have to press into His presence and stay there until we have all the grace we need to walk in victory.

That's what Jesus did in the Garden of Gethsemane. He was facing the darkest hour of his life. He

---

[141] NASB

was about to experience an agony we can't even imagine. The pressure of it caused Him to literally sweat drops of blood. Fully aware that He needed supernatural strength to do what God was requiring of Him, Jesus said to His disciples, "Sit here while I go on ahead to pray." Then...

> Grace is God's supernatural ability that empowers us to do what we cannot do on our own.

>> He took Peter and Zebedee's two sons, James and John, and he began to be filled with anguish and deep distress. He told them, "My soul is crushed with grief to the point of death. Stay here and watch with me." He went on a little farther and fell face down on the ground, praying, "My Father! If it is possible, let this cup of suffering be taken away from me. Yet I want your will, not mine." Then he returned to the disciples and found them asleep...Again he left them and prayed, "My Father! If this cup cannot be taken away until I drink it, your will be done." He returned to them again and found them sleeping, for they just couldn't keep their eyes open. So he went back to pray a third time, saying the same things again (Matthew 26:36-40, 42-44).

Notice, Jesus prayed the same prayer three times. He kept fellowshipping with His Heavenly Father until He received the divine empowerment He needed to go to the cross.

Once He received that empowerment, Jesus was like a different man. He was no longer stressed and heavy hearted. He arose from His place of prayer full of peace and ready to fulfill God's will. "Up, let's be going,"[142] He said to His disciples. Then without flinching, He turned to the soldiers who'd come to arrest Him and greeted them with words that were so full of supernatural power they knocked the entire battalion backward onto the ground!

GET THE BETTER END OF THE DEAL

That same kind of supernatural power is available to us. When we're facing difficult situations, when we've been hurt or betrayed, if we'll draw near to the throne of grace, God will give us the strength we need to forgive. He'll fill us with His peace and comfort our hearts. He'll keep the promise Jesus made in Luke 10:19:

> "Behold, I give you the authority to trample on serpents and scorpions, and over all the power of the enemy, and nothing shall by any means hurt you."[143]

That's an awesome promise! It can set us free once and for all from the fear of mistreatment. It can enable us to let go of all bitterness about the past and look toward the future with absolute confidence, declaring,

---
[142] v. 46
[143] NKJV

"Nothing shall harm me! I'm in control of my feelings, my responses, and my decisions. No matter what anybody around me does, I will choose to forgive. I will keep obeying and believing God and I'll be better off next year than I am this year because I'm walking in His blessings."

Personally, I've made that declaration many times. It's what kept me from getting bitter when, on two different occasions, I had financial inheritances stolen from me. Instead of getting angry about it, I drew near to the Lord and trusted Him to protect me. He reminded of Proverbs 6:31 that says, "A thief...when he is found must restore sevenfold."

Cool! I thought. *The people who stole from me only got one inheritance. But if I'll stand in faith on the Word, God will give me seven times more."*

Who got the better end of the deal?

I did.

So I didn't have to fret over what those people did to me. I was content to let them have the little inheritance they got. I let them fight over it among themselves and refused to get involved because I knew that regardless of what they did to me, I'd end up the winner.

The same can be true for you. If you'll forgive the people who've done you wrong and put your faith in God, He'll always bring you out on top. He'll cause every betrayal to bring you greater blessings.

If you want to see an example of how He does it, read what the Bible says about Jacob. He knew a lot about being swindled! He was cheated by his father-in-law, Laban, for 20 years.

I won't take the time to tell you everything, but a nutshell, here's what happened.

Laban promised Jacob that if he worked for him for seven years, he could marry Laban's youngest daughter, Rebecca who was the love of his life. But on the wedding night, Laban pulled a switch. He gave Jacob his older daughter, Leah. Then Jacob worked another seven years for Rebecca.

Once the 14 years were up, Jacob continued working for his father-in-law (Why? I don't know!) and Laban continued to con him, changing his wages 10 times. Through it all, Jacob held his peace. He didn't get mad. He didn't get into strife. He just kept trusting God.

Sure enough, God came through for him. He visited Jacob in a dream and gave him a supernatural plan. He told him to ask for all the spotted, speckled, and streaked animals from Laban's flocks as his wages.

Laban agreed to the plan, but then tried to cheat Jacob again by removing all such animals from his flocks so that only the solid colored ones were left.

Just when it looked as though Jacob would never come out ahead, at the leading of the Lord:

> Jacob took fresh shoots from poplar, almond, and plane trees and peeled off strips of the bark to make white streaks on them. Then he set up these peeled branches beside the watering

troughs so Laban's flocks would see them as they came to drink, for that was when they mated. So when the flocks mated in front of the white-streaked branches, all of their offspring were streaked, speckled, and spotted. Jacob added them to his own flock, thus separating the lambs from Laban's flock. Then at mating time, he turned the flocks toward the streaked and dark-colored rams in Laban's flock. This is how he built his flock from Laban's. As a result, Jacob's flocks increased rapidly, and he became very wealthy, with many servants, camels, and donkeys (Genesis 30:37-40, 43).

In the end, no matter how hard Laban tried, he couldn't stop his son-in-law from being blessed. He could not rob Jacob of this testimony: "The God of my father has been with me. He has not allowed my enemy to do me any harm."

> Leaving the place of weeping behind, you can go on from strength to strength, to the place where bitterness is banished, prayers are answered, and destinies thrive.

That can be your testimony too.

You don't have to be stuck in the Valley of Baca. Like Jacob, you can get moving again. You can go boldly to the throne of grace and receive the supernatural ability to forgive others as God has forgiven you.

Leaving the place of weeping behind, you can go on from strength to strength, to the place where bitterness is banished, prayers are answered, and destinies thrive. That's the place of blessing. And when you get there, you'll want to settle down and make it your home because it's a fabulous place to live.

13

GUARD YOUR HEART

Because of the miraculous signs he did in Jerusalem at the Passover celebration, many people were convinced that he was indeed the Messiah. But Jesus didn't trust them, because he knew what people were really like. No one needed to tell him about human nature.
(John 2:23-25)

"Forgive...but *never* forget."

For a moment, nobody at the Women's Conference could believe I'd actually said it. Out loud. In church. From the platform.

I waited as my words had their intended effect and a wave of shock rippled through the room. The pretty Christian faces that had looked at me so brightly when the meeting started began clouding over. This was not what they'd expected to hear. Especially after the nice,

Biblical message on forgiveness I'd preached the previous night.

In the awkward pause that followed, they shifted in their seats. Hoping I'd simply misspoken, they waited for me correct myself.

When I didn't, one of them spoke up. She was confident I'd simply fallen prey to a slip of the tongue. Eager to help me out, she smiled and said, "You mean, forgive and forget."

"No." I replied. "Forgive and *never* forget."

Still smiling but determined to straighten out either my phrasing or my doctrine (whichever might be the problem) the woman persisted. "Forgive and forget!" she said, this time with more authority.

"No." I repeated. "Forgive and *never* forget."

I'd chosen the words on purpose. Although I knew they'd initially be misunderstood, I wanted to provoke the group a little. I wanted to get these women thinking. To rattle their religious preconceptions so they'd never forget the point I was about to make, which was this:

God not only requires us to forgive people who mistreat us, He also commands us to wise up and protect ourselves so that we don't end up living like perpetual victims—being mistreated over...and over... and over again.

"What?!" you might say. "That's not scriptural! The Bible doesn't tell us to protect ourselves."

Yes it does. It says very clearly, "Above all else, guard your heart, for it affects everything you do."[144]

Guard your heart. That's a direct command. And obeying it involves more than just staying away from X-rated movies and other sinful stuff. It involves exercising wisdom in our relationships. If we're truly going to guard our heart, we must stop setting ourselves up for repeated disappointment, hurt, anger, and offense. Which means we must stop giving untrustworthy people unrestricted access to us.

I realize that's a foreign concept to many believers. They think there's something inherently unchristian about putting up any kind of boundaries to keep themselves safe. They have the idea that because the Bible teaches us to love everyone, we must keep the door of our heart and life wide open all the time, even to people who habitually mistreat us.

> If we're truly going to guard our heart, we must stop setting ourselves up for repeated disappointment, hurt, anger, and offense.

But that's not scriptural. The Bible tells us to be loving not foolish—and it's foolish to turn a blind eye to potential dangers. It's foolish to ignore people's character flaws. Proverbs 22:3 says, "A prudent person foresees danger and takes precautions. The simpleton goes blindly on and suffers the consequences."

---

[144] Proverbs 4:23

Forgiving someone for wronging us "seventy times seven," as Jesus said, doesn't mean we must forget what that person's character and behavior patterns reveal about them. It doesn't mean we must expose ourselves to additional, unnecessary harm by treating repeat offenders as if they're never going to hurt us again.

That can be a major mistake. It can leave us feeling wounded and stupid.

Like the turtle in the little fable I once heard.

As the story goes, the turtle let a scorpion ride on his back one day when he swam across the river. He should have known better. He'd seen how wickedly the scorpion had used his tail in the past. But (being a Christian turtle, I suppose) he chose to think the best about the scorpion and treat him like a friend.

The turtle's foolishness became apparent when the pair reached the other side of the river. Instead of thanking the turtle for the ride, the scorpion promptly stung him.

"I was kind to you!" cried the turtle. "Why did you sting me?"

"Because that's who I am," the scorpion replied.

Too bad that turtle hadn't learned how to forgive and never forget. He would have acted with more wisdom and his story would have ended better. He would have loved the scorpion from a safer distance and spared himself a great deal of pain.

BE LOVING AND BEWARE AT THE SAME TIME

Why is it so important for us, as believers, to protect our heart from needless pain?

Because, according to Jesus, our heart is the spiritual soil where the seed of God's Word is planted. Just as the condition of natural soil determines how well the crop that's planted in it will produce, the condition of our heart determines how much fruit the seed of the Word will bear in our lives.

In the parable of the sower in Mark 4, Jesus explained it this way:

> A farmer went out to plant some seed. As he scattered it across his field, some seed fell on a footpath, and the birds came and ate it. Other seed fell on shallow soil with underlying rock. The plant sprang up quickly, but it soon wilted beneath the hot sun and died because the roots had no nourishment in the shallow soil. Other seed fell among thorns that shot up and choked out the tender blades so that it produced no grain. Still other seed fell on fertile soil and produced a crop that was thirty, sixty, and even a hundred times as much as had been planted (vv. 3-8).

Notice that three of the four types of soil Jesus mentioned there were unfruitful. Of those three, the most unproductive was what He called the "footpath." A footpath is soil that's been walked on. It's been trampled by people until it's hard.

What does the footpath in the parable represent?

Jesus said it "represents those who hear the message, but then Satan comes at once and takes it away from them."[145]

I don't want to be one of those people, do you? I don't want the devil to be able to steal God's Word from me as soon as I hear it. I want the Word to take root in me and bear lots of good fruit!

That's why I'm so determined to diligently guard my heart. I know what can happen if I leave it unprotected so that just anybody who wants to can come tramping through. I've seen the results of that kind of trespassing.

I've known Christians who've been walked on almost all their lives. Maybe when they were children their parents abused them. Maybe their spouse was abusive and they didn't know what to do about it. Maybe they were mistreated by other loved ones or simply felt that life had handed them one hard knock after another. Whatever the situation, they responded by becoming insensitive and cynical. They got tough

> Instead of exercising godly wisdom to determine who they should trust and who they should love from a safer distance, they walled themselves off and kept everybody out.

---

[145] Mark 4:15

on the inside in order to prevent anyone from doing them damage again.

Instead of exercising godly wisdom to determine who they should trust and who they should love from a safer distance, they walled themselves off and kept everybody out. They lost their ability to sift out the bad relationships and retain the good. They began to resist everything—including God—for the sake of protection.

I understand how that happens. I realize there are reasons why people let their hearts get hard. But though there are reasons, there is no excuse. We must always resist hard-heartedness.

If our hearts have been calloused by hurts from the past, we must forgive and receive the grace God offers us so that we can become tender-hearted and sensitive again. We must allow God's love to open us to right relationships with others and, most importantly, with Him. Then we must take the responsibility He has given us and guard our hearts by managing those relationships wisely.

Like Jesus managed His.

Jesus did manage His relationships, you know. Contrary to popular belief, He didn't treat everybody the same. Although He loved everyone, He only brought a few people into His inner circle of friends. The others He related to in differing ways, depending on which of these four categories they fell into: Adders, Subtracters, Multipliers, or Dividers.

I know it may sound clinical to divide people up in that way, but the fact is every person in our life fits in one of those categories. The Adders and Multipliers have a godly influence on us because, like God, they help us increase. They add joy, wisdom, encouragement, or some other good thing to our life. The more Adder and Multiplier friends we have the more we will flourish and grow.

Subtracters and Dividers, on the other hand, bring trouble. Our relationships with them drag us down. Like the scorpion who rode the turtle, they take from us and then sting us.

Subtracters and Dividers usually get access to us either through guilt and manipulation ("If you were really a Christian, you'd be here for me when I need you!"), or by appealing to our flesh ("Stick with me and I'll make sure you get that promotion.") Sometimes they'll offer us juicy tidbits of gossip as bait. Promising us the inside scoop, they'll convince us that being close to them will keep us "in the know."

That's the same tactic Satan used with Eve. He promised her knowledge. When she took him up on his offer, she lost everything. Think about that the next time a Divider sidles up to you and whispers, "Hey, did you hear about what so-and-so got caught doing last night?"

Say, "No, I didn't. And what's more, I don't want to. God bless you and goodbye!" Then, exercise wisdom and walk away. Give your flesh a decent burial and get on with your life.

That's what Jesus did with the Subtracters and Dividers in His life—people like the Pharisees and Sadducees. He didn't spend much time with them. He never purposely treated them rudely but He didn't make them His friends, either. He kept His guard up high when was around them and, as we've noted time and again, He warned His disciples to do the same. "Beware of their yeast!" He said.

If we want to be wise, we'll remember those words and do what Jesus did. We'll quietly identify the Subtracters and Dividers around us. And, endeavoring to be both gracious and guarded in our relationships with them, we'll learn how to be loving and beware at the same time.

FAIR WEATHER FOLLOWERS MAKE FAIR WEATHER FRIENDS

Actually, Jesus taught us by example not to only protect ourselves from those who would harm us, but to exercise discretion in other relationships as well. In His own life and ministry He separated the people who followed Him and professed to be His friends into five different groups.

The group the Bible refers to as "the multitudes" were fair weather followers. They wanted to hear what Jesus had to say and receive from Him—but only on their own terms. They weren't really interested in being disciples. Jesus loved them and ministered to them as the Father directed but He didn't share the intimacies of His heart with them. He didn't set Himself up for disappointment by expecting them to be loyal to Him.

Even though multitudes were convinced by the miraculous signs Jesus did that He was the Messiah, "Jesus didn't trust them, because he knew what people were really like. No one needed to tell him about human nature."[146]

It's not that Jesus was cynical about the multitudes. He wasn't. He was just realistic. He knew where they were at in their relationship with Him. So He related to them accordingly. Instead of resenting them for their lack of commitment, He did what He could for them and reserved His confidences for more trustworthy groups of friends.

One of those groups was what the Bible calls "the 70." They not only had faith in Jesus as the Messiah and wanted to receive from Him, they wanted to serve Him. Interested in more than just what they could get from Him, they volunteered to be an active part of what He was doing on the earth. So His relationship with them was quite different from his relationship with the multitudes.

Jesus chose the 70 to be part of His extended His ministry team. Sending them ahead of Him in pairs to all the towns and villages He planned to visit, these were his instructions to them: "The harvest is so great, but the workers are so few. Pray to the Lord who is in charge of the harvest, and ask him to send out more workers for his fields. Go now, and remember that I

---

[146] John 2:23-25

am sending you out as lambs among wolves…heal the sick. As you heal them, say, 'The Kingdom of God is near you now.'"[147]

Think of it! Out of the thousands who showed up for Jesus' ministry meetings, He found only 70 who could be trusted to participate with Him at this level. That's a relatively small group. But we shouldn't be surprised. We see the same thing in the Church today.

> Think of it! Out of the thousands who showed up for Jesus' ministry meetings, He found only 70 who could be trusted to participate with Him at this level.

Even though every believer, deep in their heart, desires to serve God in a meaningful way, most never do it. In the majority of churches approximately 20% of the members do 90% of the work. The remaining 80%, despite frequent pleas from the pulpit for help, refuse to roll up their sleeves and commit.

In the end, people can't be forced to serve Jesus.

Real service, like true friendship, must come from the heart.

DON'T BE SHOCKED WHEN YOUR 70 LEAVE YOU

Although Jesus had a closer relationship with the 70 than with the multitudes, He still guarded His heart when He was around them. They weren't willing

---
[147] Luke 10:1-3, 9

to stand with Him through the hard times, and He knew it. So He didn't count them among His closest friends.

That's why He wasn't shocked by how they reacted to one of His sermons. He'd anticipated what their response would be when He said:

> All who eat my flesh and drink my blood remain in me, and I in them. I live by the power of the living Father who sent me; in the same way, those who partake of me will live because of me. I am the true bread from heaven. Anyone who eats this bread will live forever and not die as your ancestors did, even though they ate the manna (John 6:56-58).

> *Jesus, because He was a God-pleaser not a people-pleaser, was unfazed by their criticism. He didn't try to appease them by compromising His message.*

Many of the 70 decided that message was too radical for them. "This is very hard to understand. How can anyone accept it?"[148] they cried.

Jesus, because He was a God-pleaser not a people-pleaser, was unfazed by their criticism. He didn't try to appease them by compromising His message or backing off from the Word of God. Instead, He made them even more upset.

---
[148] v. 60

"Does this offend you?" He said. "Then what will you think if you see me, the Son of Man, return to heaven again? It is the Spirit who gives eternal life. Human effort accomplishes nothing. And the very words I have spoken to you are spirit and life."[149]

Since that wasn't what the 70 wanted to hear, "at this point many of his disciples turned away and deserted him."[150] But Jesus didn't respond to their departure like Christians today probably would. He didn't cry and feel rejected. He didn't get angry and accuse the 70 of betraying Him or vow never to trust anyone again. On the contrary, He stayed perfectly calm. He didn't even seem surprised about what had happened.

What was the secret to His composure?

He'd already identified the nature of His relationship with these people. He knew what category they fell into. Aware that their commitment to Him was conditional, He wasn't caught off guard when they abandoned Him. He didn't suffer any unnecessary hurt.

Truth be told, He took the response of the 70 so much in stride that after they left, He turned to the 12 and asked, "Are you going to leave, too?"[151]

They didn't, of course, because they were a more unique group. The 12 had chosen to enter into a deeper level of partnership and fellowship with the Lord. They walked with Him every day. Having committed themselves completely to Him, they stuck with Him

---

[149] vv. 61-64
[150] v. 66
[151] v. 67

even through the uncomfortable times. They were determined to be faithful to Him at any cost.

The 12 disciples represented only a tiny fraction of the people Jesus knew and loved, yet they were the only ones on earth that had almost unrestricted access to Him. They could talk to Him anytime they wanted. They could depend on Him to be there for them in every time of need. And He depended on them as well (to some extent) even though they sometimes failed Him.

From that group of 12, Jesus selected another group of three—Peter, James, and John—to be even closer to Him. He shared with them, and only them, the most sacred moments of His life and ministry. They were present on the Mount of Transfiguration. They were there when He raised Jairus' daughter from the dead. They were with Him in the Garden of Gethsemane when He was praying as if His heart would break.

> Because John understood better than anyone else just how much Jesus loved him, he had a greater capacity to love others.

Ultimately, from those three, Jesus chose one who would be nearest and dearest to him: John, the disciple who referred to himself again and again as "the one that Jesus loved."[152] Because John understood better than anyone else just how much Jesus loved him, he

---

[152] John 13:23; 19:26; 20:2; 21:7, 20

had a greater capacity to love others. His kindness and unconditional commitment earned him a position of such trust with the Lord that on the cross Jesus gave him the responsibility of caring for His mother.

In His greatest hour of need, it seems that John was the one person Jesus could completely trust.

A WISE WAY TO LIVE

I realize all this may upset some people's religious traditions but, as we've just seen, this is the reality: Although Jesus loved and forgave everybody who ever mistreated Him (including the Pharisees, the multitudes, and the 70) He did not forget about their character flaws and patterns of behavior. He did not embrace them all as His closest friends.

Jesus—though He was perfectly loving, unselfish, merciful, forgiving, and gracious—put up appropriate boundaries in His relationships with people. He refused to allow abusers, casual curiosity seekers, fair-weather followers, and double-minded disciples to trample on His heart at will. Instead, He gave different groups of people different levels of access to Him. Some He kept at a distance while others He brought close, depending on which of the five types of followers they chose to be.

That's a wise way to live. As believers, we should learn a lesson from it. We should start evaluating the various relationships in our lives and (with the help of the Holy Spirit) determine what kind they are.

As we do, we'll realize that most of our acquaintances fit into the category of the multitude. They're more than willing to take what we give them but they don't want to reciprocate. They call us when they're facing an emergency, but otherwise they're nowhere to be found.

Once we identify the multitude people in our life, we won't be shocked or offended by how they treat us. We'll know in advance not to expect much from them. Instead of resenting them, we can relate to them like the Master related to the multitudes in His life. We can minister to them as the Lord leads, while maintaining a safe emotional distance.

Other people in our lives fit into the category of the 70. Willing to engage in a more reciprocal relationship, they aren't just interested in pursuing their own personal gain. They want to add value to our life... as long as it doesn't inconvenience them or cost them too much. Such 70-type friends can be a blessing. We can enjoy a certain measure of closeness to them. But we should always keep in mind that their commitment to us will crumble under pressure. When things get difficult, they'll most likely choose to hit the road.

We'll find that our 12-type friends, by contrast, are far more dependable. We can let our guard down much more with them. They share our commitment to the Lord and are eager to serve with us side-by-side as we work in His Kingdom. They'll not only call on us when things get tough in their lives, they'll be there for us in hard times too.

Some of those friends may become as close to us as Jesus' three closest disciples were to Him. They'll earn our trust (and we'll earn theirs) to such a degree that we'll be able to lean on them during our most vulnerable moments. We'll share with them our greatest joys and spiritual revelations. And when we find ourselves weeping in a Garden of Gethsemane, they'll be there with us, praying by our side.

If we're truly blessed, we may even have a friend who, like John, becomes so dear and faithful that we can call on them for anything. A friend who will gladly take on the responsibility of loving us and our family, of caring for us in times of crisis. A "real friend" who, as the Bible says it, "sticks closer than a brother."[153]

> And when we find ourselves weeping in a Garden of Gethsemane, they'll be there with us, praying by our side.

Let me be clear. I don't mean to say that friendships should be categorized rigidly and never changed. Some people in your life may move from one kind of friend to another. A 70-type friend might mature in character and in relationship with the Lord and become someone you can depend on without question. They might become one of your three.

You might have another friend where just the opposite is true. A relationship that was once close might become more distant. A friend who's been near to you for years might begin to stray from his walk

---
[153] Proverbs 18:24

with the Lord, for instance. Rather than encouraging you in your Christian life, he might become a negative influence. As a result, you'll have to put distance between you. You'll have to relate to him as one of the multitude.

"Are you saying I can't have close friends who are unsaved or in a backslidden condition?"

Yes. That's exactly what I'm saying.

"Bad company corrupts good character."[154] So if you want to keep moving forward with Jesus, you can't afford to associate closely with people who are going the other way. You can continue to love them and encourage them when you have the opportunity, but you can't make them part of your inner circle of friends.

Jesus said, "Wide is the gate and broad is the way that leads to destruction, and there are many who go in by it."[155] If you're walking with a friend who chooses the broad path and you don't part ways with them, you may wind up on the road to destruction too.

> Every day we are choosing either to obey God's Word or to ignore it, to move toward our destiny in Christ or away from it.

Every day we stand at the crossroads. Every day we are choosing either to obey God's Word or to ignore it, to move toward our destiny in Christ or away from it.

---

[154] 1 Corinthians 15:33
[155] Matthew 7:13-14, NKJV

Choosing to go with God will separate us from people who've chosen otherwise. It will cost us some friendships. But in the end, we'll be glad we paid the price. We'll be glad we chose, above all, to guard our heart.

14

BE BOLD AND KEEP BUILDING!

Sanballat was very angry when he learned that we were rebuilding the wall. He flew into a rage and mocked the Jews, saying in front of his friends and the Samarian army officers, "What does this bunch of poor, feeble Jews think they are doing? Do they think they can build the wall?"
(Nehemiah 4:1-2)

Let me warn you in advance: the devil won't like it when you start guarding your heart. He won't just stand by and watch while you put healthy boundaries in place. He'll fight you over them. He'll accuse you of being selfish, un-Christ-like, unforgiving, and rebellious. Determined to push you back into the role of helpless, mistreated, victim, he'll do his best to make you feel guilty for standing up for yourself.

He's not the only one who will do it, either.

The people in your life who've grown accustomed to your lack of boundaries in the past will chime in too. They won't like it when you change the rules of the game. Especially if you've allowed them to take advantage of you or mistreat you for a significant period of time, they're almost sure to condemn you and cry, "Foul!"

In other words, they'll do to you the same thing people did to Nehemiah in the Old Testament. When he returned to Jerusalem to rebuild the city walls, the local Gentiles who lived in the region had an absolute fit. They acted as if the resurrection of Jerusalem's boundaries was a personal assault.

Why were they so upset?

Because they'd been accustomed to tramping through the ruined city and taking whatever they wanted. They'd treated it as if it belonged to them. What's more, they knew that if Nehemiah's rebuilding project succeeded, the Jews would regain their dominion and fulfill their God-ordained destiny.

Talk about opposition! Nehemiah and his team stirred up a real hornet's nest when they went to work on that wall. Their enemies—men named Sanballat, Tobiah, and Geshem the Arab—protested, accused, and threatened them. "When [they] heard of our plan, they scoffed contemptuously," said Nehemiah. "'What are you doing, rebelling against the king like this?' they asked."[156]

How Nehemiah responded to their taunts is well worth remembering. It can help us when the devil is lobbing similar accusations at us. "The God of heaven will help us succeed," he replied. "We his servants will start rebuilding this wall. But you have no stake or claim in Jerusalem."[157]

Nehemiah knew, without question, that the property of Jerusalem belonged to him and his fellow Jews. He also knew that it did *not* belong to anybody else. Such knowledge, simple as it sounds, is vital when it comes to setting boundaries.

> How Nehemiah responded to their taunts is well worth remembering. It can help us when the devil is lobbing similar accusations at us.

That's why home owners have property lines around their land. They need to be able to define what is and is not theirs. Since they're responsible for what happens on their property and they're not responsible for what happens on anybody else's, they must know where their legal authority begins and ends. If a home owner is unclear about his property lines, he can go to the courthouse and obtain legal documents that make the boundaries clear.

---

[156] Nehemiah 2:19
[157] v. 20

The same principles can be applied by each one of us to our own life.

Our life is our God-given property and God has given us the freedom to do whatever we choose with it. He's established invisible property lines that define what is and is not our responsibility, and where we do and do not have authority. The property lines of our life identify where we end and someone else begins.

If we're going to be spiritually healthy and free to fulfill our destiny, we must know where those lines are. We must find out from the Word how to protect them, and do it without apology.

That's what Nehemiah did. When people got upset with him for building a wall around Jerusalem, he didn't apologize. He knew that He'd been divinely commanded to guard that property, so he faced his accusers with confidence and refused to back down.

How can you and I develop that kind of confidence? How can we be as sure as Nehemiah was that building healthy boundaries around our lives is the right thing to do?

By looking at our Heavenly Father.

The Bible tells us to "Be imitators of God [copy Him and follow His example], as well-beloved children [imitate their father]."[158] So if God has boundaries, then we can be certain that we should have them too. And there's no question about it, God has *lots* of boundaries.

First of all, He has personal boundaries. He is a distinct Being, separate from His creation and from mankind. He defines His identity for us in the Scriptures, telling us Who He is and Who He is not. He says, for instance, that He is love and He is light; that there is no darkness in Him.[159] He's not the tempter and He never tempts with evil.[160]

God even defines for us the three members of the Trinity, letting us know that each is His own Person with His own distinct responsibilities. The Father is the Creator and sustainer of our life. The Son is our elder Brother, Savior, and Friend. The Holy Spirit is our Helper, Teacher and Comforter.

God also distinguishes between His responsibilities and ours. He says to us time and again in various ways, "If you diligently obey and keep My commandments, I will see to it that My blessings overtake you."

He also confronts us when we disobey those commandments. (Remember how God sent the prophet, Nathan, to confront David about his adultery with Bathsheba?) He appoints consequences for our behavior and sets limits on what He is willing to allow in His house. He doesn't try to control people, He simply says, "If you choose to do evil, I will permit you to do

---
[158] Ephesians 5:1, AMP
[159] 1 John 4:16; 1:6
[160] James 1:13

so, but I will not permit you to bring that evil into My presence."

Just as Jerusalem had property lines in Nehemiah's day and those lines were marked by walls that had gates which opened and closed to keep bad things out and good things in, God has property lines too. He has a divine fence with gates that swing both ways. They close to keep evil from getting into His presence, yet they open to allow His love to continually flow out to everyone. God's gates keep unrepentant unbelievers out and yet provide an entrance so that whosoever will receive Jesus can come in and fellowship with Him.

A CONFRONTATIONAL MESSAGE

We can see just by looking at our physical bodies that God created us to have boundaries just like He does. He has separated us physically from the earthly elements around us by a boundary called *skin*. It's designed to keep out bad things like germs and infection while keeping in the good things like our blood, bones, and organs. Like all healthy boundaries, our skin is permeable. It has gates, so to speak. They give entrance to the good things in our environment and provide an exit for the toxins inside us that need to get out.

Most of us (unless we were physically abused) instinctively understand that our body is our property. We know that we have the right to say no when someone tries to trespass on it. As good parents, we teach our children that if anyone attempts to touch their body inappropriately, they should refuse to allow it, and they should take action by telling a parent, a teacher, or the police.

Sounds like basic logic, doesn't it? Just good, godly, common sense.

Yet so many times we fail to exercise the same wisdom in guarding other areas of our life. We hesitate to confront someone for violating the boundaries of our soul. We're reluctant to say to someone who's mistreated us, "No! I don't want you to do it anymore. And if you continue I'm going to take appropriate action to protect myself."

I know what you're thinking.

Vikki, it's one thing to beware of untrustworthy people, like we talked about in the last chapter, but it's another to actually do something about their mistreatment. Aren't we supposed to be longsuffering with each other? Aren't we supposed to bear with each other's weaknesses?

Yes, we are. But that doesn't mean we should allow people to sin against us, to violate, or mistreat us in any area of life without experiencing any consequences for their behavior. Jesus made that clear. He even preached a sermon about it. He said:

> If another believer sins against you, go privately and point out the fault. If the other person listens and confesses it, you have won that person back. But if you are unsuccessful, take one or two others with you and go back again, so that everything you say may be

confirmed by two or three witnesses. If that person still refuses to listen, take your case to the church. If the church decides you are right, but the other person won't accept it, treat that person as a pagan or a corrupt tax collector (Matthew 18:15-17).

Any way you cut it, that's a confrontational message. And it's not one we generally hear a lot in church these days. Maybe that's one of the reasons so many Christians have trouble staying free of resentment and bitterness. They don't know God actually wants them to put up appropriately gated fences around their hearts and their lives. They don't realize He has given them permission to say, "No."

NO TRESPASSING: VIOLATORS WILL BE PROSECUTED

I mean that literally.

Saying no, in one form or another, is the key to guarding the property God has entrusted to us. Words are boundary setters. That's why the Bible tells us, "Say a simple, 'Yes, I will,' or 'No, I won't.' Your word is enough."[161]

If we don't tell people what we are willing to accept and what we aren't, they won't know. They'll trample all over our boundaries without even realizing it.

Think of a fence with a sign on it that says, *No Trespassing: Violators Will Be Prosecuted*. Saying no is like putting up one of those signs. It helps other

---
[161] Matthew 5:37

people identify our boundaries and lets them know the consequences they can expect if they transgress them. It communicates to people what kind of behavior is acceptable to us and establishes limits on mistreatment or abuse.

Most of us, however, are uncomfortable with saying no. We're concerned it will upset people. And the idea of setting and enforcing consequences? We're hesitant that might be downright wrong. So when we start to do it, the boundary-violators in our lives will usually prey on those fears. Egged on by the devil, they'll try to put a guilt trip on us. They'll threaten us (emotionally, if not physically) hoping we'll cave in and let them go right on treating us any way they want without any repercussions.

When that happens, we should simply do to others what God does to us when we want to sin without consequences.

Using His Word to set boundaries, He tells us clearly what He likes and what He doesn't. He sets limits and notifies us that there will be consequences to violating them. He explains to us very clearly that if we walk one way one thing will happen and if we walk another way another thing will happen. Again and again throughout the Bible He says:

- If you live according to the flesh you will die; but if by the Spirit you put to death the deeds of the body, you will live (Romans 8:13).
- He who sows to his flesh will of the flesh reap corruption, but he who sows to the Spirit will of the Spirit reap everlasting life (Galatians 6:8, NKJV).
- If anyone will not work, neither shall he eat... He who has a slack hand becomes poor, but the hand of the diligent makes rich (2 Thessalonians 3:10, Proverbs 10:4 NKJV).
- When you follow the desires of your sinful nature, your lives will produce these evil results: sexual immorality, impure thoughts, eagerness for lustful pleasure...and other kinds of sin... Anyone living that sort of life will not inherit the Kingdom of God (Galatians 5:19, 21).

Just imagine how many marriages could be saved if Christian wives or husbands would act more like God by setting limits and following through with consequences! Think how much pain, bitterness, and mistreatment could be avoided if believers who were being abused would say, "If you don't stop drinking, or hitting me, or hurting the kids, I will... [insert the appropriate consequence: i.e. contact your family and ask them to intervene, leave, or call the police]."

Although such consequences are never greeted with enthusiasm by the people they affect, they're crucial. They're like the barbed wire in your fence. They reflect the seriousness of the trespass and communicate your self-respect. They let others know you're willing to do whatever is necessary to guard your heart and your life.

Sadly, however, relatively few Christians choose to take that kind of stand. Instead, they passively put up with all kinds violations. Saying yes when they mean no, they give control of their property to others, all the while resenting it inside and getting ever more deeply mired in the trap of offense.

DON'T IGNORE YOUR EMOTIONAL BAROMETER

Some believers hesitate to confront people who mistreat them because they simply don't know where to draw the line. They feel as if they've been put in the middle of an open field and instructed to diligently guard it—without being told what the property parameters are.

Have I been given an acre? Two acres? Or a square mile? they wonder. *How can I know if somebody is trespassing if I have no idea where the borders of my property are?*

They can't, of course. That's why they're frequently confused and frustrated in their relationships with other people. They struggle with anger, agitation, and hurt, sensing in their heart that they're being run over in some way. But because they're not sure where their personal property lines are, they can't be certain a trespass has been committed. So instead of dealing with the problem, they simply try to suppress their emotions and "be nice."

While we should never allow our emotions to dominate us in any situation, emotions have gotten a bad rap in Christian circles. They've been written off as fleshly or carnal. We've gotten the idea they're just pesky, insignificant remnants of our fallen humanity that must be either squashed or ignored.

But our emotions are given to us by God! He created us to experience the same kinds of feelings He does—including compassion, joy, sadness, and even anger.

As long as we keep our emotions under control (one of the fruit of the spirit is self-control) they can be extremely beneficial. They can move us to take positive action, as in the case of the good Samaritan, for example. His compassion moved him to take care of the wounded man he encountered on the road to Jericho.

> Emotions can also serve as a relational barometer. Loving, happy feelings can be a signal that all is well. Negative feelings, can indicate there's a problem.

Emotions can also serve as a relational barometer. Loving, happy feelings can be a signal that all is well. Negative feelings, on the other hand, can indicate there's a problem. Much like the pain we feel when we touch a hot stove tells us to pull back our hand and avoid further injury, painful emotions can warn us that we're being violated some way.

We need to pay attention to such warnings. Doing otherwise can be dangerous. Years of ignoring depression can lead to suicide. Years of suppressing anger can lead to health problems. Our emotions are our responsibility and we should be attentive to them and respond to them correctly.

Which brings us back to knowing where to draw the line.

Our emotions can be very helpful in that area. They can send us signals that indicate our God-appointed boundaries are being transgressed. They can alert us to the fact that something is wrong. Then we can look to the Word and find out what we should do about it.

Let me give you a simple example. Say, for instance, Believer Bob gets a call from a fellow Christian who is facing a crisis. He needs a ride to work because his car is in the shop for repairs. He has an important meeting that he can't afford to miss. If he doesn't show up, he could be fired, and he hasn't been able to arrange for any other transportation.

Bob (who loves the Lord and enjoys being a blessing to people) is glad to help out. He rearranges his schedule and drives the extra miles with a happy heart because he senses the Lord leading him to help this brother.

But what if the brother keeps requesting rides day after day? What if he says he can't afford the repairs on his car and starts expecting to be chauffeured not only to work but to the grocery store and to church on Sundays?

You know as well as I do that after a few days of that, Bob (if he doesn't say no) will start feeling resentful, angry, and mistreated. He'll find himself wanting to tell his hitch-hiking brother that he must arrange for different transportation; that he needs to get his car repaired, walk to work, or take the bus.

But Bob knows better than to let his emotions run the show. So he opens his Bible to see what boundaries he should set. He reads in Galatians 6:2 that we're to "Bear...one another's burdens, and so fulfil the law of Christ."[162]

Committed to obeying the law of love, he's about to decide it would be wrong to say no to his brother in this time of need when he sees another verse in the same passage that says, "Every man shall bear his own burden."[163] *What does God want me to do?* he wonders. *Bear my brother's burden or not?*

The solution to this quandary can be found in the definition of the two Greek words that are translated *burden* in those verses. The first word, *baros*, refers to an extra heavy, crushing weight. It speaks of a situation so dire or a pressure so great (such a death, a critical illness, or other catastrophic calamity) that one person can't handle it alone. He must have help to make it through.

That's the kind of burden God expects us to help each other carry. He expects us to make sacrifices if

---

[162] KJV
[163] v. 8

necessary and step in to give our support when another believer is staggering under an unbearable load.

The second word, *phortion*, refers to a much lighter burden. It speaks of the everyday kind of cargo, like a backpack, that can be reasonably managed by one individual. Those kinds of burdens, the normal responsibilities of life we all have, should be handled by each individual believer. As the Bible says, "Each man shall bear his own load."

I like to say it this way: We're responsible *to* each other to help and bless as God leads. But we're each responsible *for* ourselves.

That means, in this situation, Believer Bob is not required to bear the responsibility of giving his carless fellow Christian continual rides. He can choose to draw the line. He can say, "No," guilt free and escape the trap of offense.

BIKINIS AND BEING LATE

Although Bob's story is made up, I could tell you any number of others from real life. Take, for instance, the time a friend of mine who is a pastor's wife found her boundaries being challenged in a very different way. Some members of her church kept violating her privacy by asking her prying questions. She asked me what I thought about the situation. I assured her that her role as the pastor's wife didn't obligate her to tell them everything they wanted to know.

Encouraging her to be gracious but firm in drawing the line, I shared with her a little technique I call *The*

Art of World Travel. It's something I developed over the years. "This is how it works," I told her. "The next time a church member asks you if you wore a bikini when you went on vacation with your husband" (Somebody really did ask her that. Can you believe it?) "just lead the conversation in a different direction.

"Say something like, 'Oh my goodness! A bikini? These days a bikini is modest compared to some of the things people wear on the beach. I mean, California beaches are one thing but last year we were on the beach in Australia which, by the way, is on the Indian Ocean. Doesn't that sound odd? Anyway, we'd gone there for a minister's conference and the people there had been so wonderful to us. I just love the Australians. We've ministered there twice just this past year. My how hungry those people are for the Lord...'"

I've used that technique to redirect lots of conversations over the years. By the time I'm finished, the focus is on an entirely different place and subject—something I'm comfortable with that doesn't violate my boundaries. My daughter, who's gotten wise to my ways, always shakes her head and smiles when someone asks me a question she knows I'm not going to answer. "I'm always interested in where we're going this time!" she says.

One of the best boundary-setters I've ever known was the pastor of the church where Dennis and I worked when we first went into ministry. He had a firm grasp on what fell within the borders of his God-given property. One of the things he knew it included was his time.

Pastor Ezell did not like to waste his time waiting for people who arrived late. So he informed all of us who worked with him what the boundaries of his property were: "To be early is to be on time," he said. "To be on time is to be late. To be late is to be left behind."

Pastor Ezell proved that you don't have to be angry to set boundaries. In fact, boundaries maintained and consequences carried out make anger unnecessary. Rather than sitting around fuming when someone was late for an outing or an event, he simply kept his plan and left on time. Those who were late were left behind—literally!

> "To be early is to be on time," he said. "To be on time is to be late. To be late is to be left behind."

What a great way to handle things! Don't get mad, don't get offended, set a boundary. Just like Pastor Ezell did.

SETTING LIMITS GOD'S WAY

"But Vikki," you might say, "do we really have the right to put limits on how other people behave?"

No, we don't. That's why it's important for us to maintain God as our example. He doesn't set limits on people or "make" them behave. He does set standards, however. He doesn't do it angrily or unkindly. He does it lovingly (and so should we). Then He lets people decide what they will do. He says:

> Today I have given you the choice between life and death, between blessings and curses. I call on heaven and earth to witness the choice you make. Oh, that you would choose life, that you and your descendants might live! (Deuteronomy 30:19).

If people choose to violate His principles and live under the curse, God lets them know, "You can behave that way if you choose, but you won't enjoy My blessing while you behave that way." Without trying to manipulate or control them in any way, God limits His exposure to evil, unrepentant people. As believers, we should do the same. We should take responsibility for guarding our hearts and lives by limiting our exposure to those who act in destructive ways.

Although drawing such lines may sometimes make us feel uncomfortable, especially in our relationships with other believers, we must do it because that's what the Bible commands. It says, "You are not to associate with anyone who claims to be a Christian yet indulges in sexual sin, or is greedy, or worships idols, or is abusive, or a drunkard, or a swindler. Don't even eat with such people."[164]

Actually, it's not just rebellious and sinful people like the ones mentioned in that verse who will try to trample over your boundaries. Good, well-meaning

---
[164] 1 Corinthians 5:11

Christians will sometimes try to run over you too. They'll come up with their own ideas about what you should be doing. They'll push you to take on responsibilities God hasn't called you to fulfill.

Like Martha did to Mary the day Jesus preached at their house. She not only put the job of cooking for the crowd ahead of listening to the Word, she decided Mary should do it too. When Mary chose to sit at Jesus' feet instead, Martha got downright upset. She even tried to convince Jesus to help her put a guilt trip on Mary in order to pressure her into to doing what Martha wanted. (Jesus refused though. He never uses guilt to motivate anybody to do anything. Guilt is the devil's tool, not God's.)

> Martha not only put the job of cooking for the crowd ahead of listening to the Word, she decided Mary should do it too.

That kind of thing happens among believers and family members all the time. They try to manipulate each other with pressure and guilt. They whine like Martha did, "You should be helping me! Don't you see how tired I am? If you were really committed to Jesus, you'd do what makes me happy."

Whenever I'm being pressured in that way by someone, I remind myself that it's not my job to make everybody happy. I'm called to be a God pleaser, not a people pleaser.

Jesus said, "Take the burden of responsibility I give you and thereby discover your life and destiny."[165] If I take on other people's responsibilities and spend all my energy trying to satisfy them, I won't have enough left over to finish my own race. So I've made up my mind to follow the leading of the Holy Spirit and do only what He tells me to do, regardless of how the people around me feel about it.

That's how Jesus lived. At times during His ministry on earth, when the multitudes pressed in upon Him and demanded Him to minister to them, He actually withdrew from them. Despite their clamoring and their great needs, He left them and went to spend time alone with His Father. To some people that might have seemed selfish. But it wasn't. It was wise. Jesus was taking time to refresh and refuel in God's presence so that, instead of wearing out, He could continue to give.

When His critics complained about how He conducted His life and ministry, He responded with a reply that, to boundary-less believers, would seem unthinkable. He said, "Your approval or disapproval means nothing to me."[166]

Jesus produced 100% results because He only did what His Father told Him to do. When other people tried to force their fleshly plans on Him, He drew the line. He said, "No."

If we want to please God like He did, we must do the same.

---

[165] Matthew 11:29, Ben Campbell Johnson Paraphrase
[166] John 5:41

It won't be easy. Setting appropriate boundaries will force us to confront all the fears that have kept us trapped in the cycle of offense. We'll have to face and conquer the fear of losing someone's love, the fear of making others angry, the fear of feeling lonely or guilty, and the fear of experiencing others' disapproval.

It will take time, courage, work, prayer, and grace to change the unhealthy relational patterns in our lives. But we owe it to the Lord to do it. After all, we're not our own, we've been bought with a price. Our life is a gift from God. He's expecting us to manage it, guard it, and make sure it brings forth fruit for His kingdom.

Like the servants in the parable Jesus told in Matthew 25, we've been entrusted with valuable treasures—our hearts, our time, our talents—to invest for our Master. If we steward them wisely, according to His will, at the end of our lives when we stand before Jesus, He'll say, "Well done, my good and faithful servant. You have been faithful in handling this small amount, so now I will give you many more responsibilities. Let's celebrate together!"[167]

> Our life is a gift from God. He's expecting us to manage it, guard it, and make sure it brings forth fruit for His kingdom.

But if we neglect that stewardship, we'll be like the wicked servant in that parable. Too afraid of the perils involved in investing his talents, he let his master's

---
[167] Matthew 25:23

treasure sit idle. So instead of being praised, he received a rebuke. His master scolded him, not for having fears, but for failing to confront and overcome them. That failure, said the master, revealed the servant's ungrateful attitude toward the gift and the giver. And it cost the servant great future rewards.

Let's not make the mistake of the unfruitful servant. Let's be bold and take good care of the property God has given us. No matter how much the enemy threatens or people complain, let's remain determined to build the boundaries that will protect us from offense and enable us to fulfill our divine destiny. As Nehemiah said, "The God of heaven will help us succeed!"

15

WILL YOU BE A SURVIVOR...OR A CHAMPION?

And from the days of John the Baptist until now the kingdom of heaven suffereth violence, and the violent take it by force.
(Matthew 11:12 KJV)

Judging purely by the t-shirts available on the internet, it's a big deal these days to be a survivor. Significant numbers of people are apparently willing to pay good money for wearable Fruit-of-the-Loom style billboards that say "I survived...." everything from hurricanes to bad hair days.

While surviving is fine (and definitely beats the alternative) I want to make this emphatically clear: It is not God's best for you. Especially when it comes to dealing with mistreatment and offense.

God has not called you to simply endure mistreatment, put up with the pain and loss the devil inflicts on you, and stagger across the finish line of life gasping, "Well, at least I survived."

No. Absolutely not.

God created you to be victor, not a survivor. He promised not only to preserve you but to avenge you of your adversary—who, I should remind you, is the devil, not people—and make you more than a conqueror in every area of life. If something has been lost or stolen from you, God wants it restored with interest. Wherever you've been wronged, He wants things made right.

"For I the Lord love justice;" He says. "I hate robbery and wrong...And I will faithfully give them their recompense."[168]

If you want to see what God's idea of recompense looks like, read about what He did when He delivered the Hebrews out of Egypt. He didn't just set them free from slavery. That alone didn't satisfy His sense of justice. The way God saw it, the Egyptians owed the Israelites big time for the years of work they'd been forced to do. So He instructed the Israelites right before they exited Egypt to ask the Egyptians for articles of silver and gold, and clothing.

> If something has been lost or stolen from you, God wants it restored with interest. Wherever you've been wronged, He wants things made right.

---

[168] Isaiah 61:8, AMP

Under ordinary circumstances, such a request would have been utterly rejected. But these were no ordinary circumstances. God, moving supernaturally on behalf of His people, "caused the Egyptians to look favorably on the Israelites, and they gave the Israelites whatever they asked for. So, like a victorious army, they plundered the Egyptians!"[169]

Think of it! Those Hebrew slaves were in bondage one day and wealthy and free the next. God's love for justice made them rich overnight.

That wasn't something God did just once, either. The Bible tells us about many such incidents.

One of my personal favorites is the one recorded in 1 Samuel 30. That chapter tells the story of how David and his warriors returned to their camp at Ziklag after fighting a battle, and found nothing but a silent, smoldering pile of ashes. Their homes were in ruins. Their wives and children gone—kidnapped by the Amalekites.

> Think of it! Those Hebrew slaves were broke and in bondage one day and wealthy and free the next.

It was a gruesome scene. Nothing and no one was left. David and his men were so stunned and grief stricken that at first all they could do was cry. The Bible says, they wept until they had no more strength to weep.

---

[169] Exodus 12:36

Personally, I'm grateful God included that fact in Scripture because sometimes when I've been hurt in an especially deep and painful way, that's what I have to do too. At first, I have to cry. David, who was a man after God's own heart, proved that's okay.

God understands when we've been blindsided by some horrific hurt that it may take us some time to process our emotions. He is compassionate and willing to help us through that process, but here's the problem: too many stop there. Once we've recovered our emotions and come to terms with what has happened, we decide to put the whole thing behind us. We just thank God that, by the grace of God, we're still alive.

But that's not what David did. He didn't try to console himself and his men (who, after they finished crying, decided this was all David's fault and started talking about stoning him) by saying, "Hey guys, look on the bright side. At least we survived!"

> Even though they were already worn out from weeping, they went after the enemy that had robbed and victimized them.

No, David knew better than that. He knew God had called him to be a champion. So, after strengthening himself in the Lord, he asked God a crucial question, "Should I pursue these enemies?"

And He answered him, "Pursue, for you shall surely overtake them and without fail recover all."[170]

---
[170] 1 Samuel 30:8

David and his men wasted no time obeying that command. Even though they were already worn out from weeping, they went after the enemy that had robbed and victimized them.

Before the day was out, they found them.

> The Amalekites were spread out across the fields, eating and drinking and dancing with joy because of the vast amount of plunder they had taken from the Philistines and the land of Judah. David and his men rushed in among them and slaughtered them throughout that night and the entire next day until evening... David got back everything the Amalekites had taken, and he rescued his two wives. Nothing was missing: small or great, son or daughter, or anything else that had been taken. David brought everything back. His troops rounded up all the flocks and herds and drove them on ahead. "These all belong to David as his reward!" they said (verses 16-20).

Now that's what I call justice! Not only did David get back everything he'd lost, he ended up with more than he had when he started. He didn't just get restored, he got a reward!

GOD IS NOT AN UNJUST JUDGE

As God's obedient children, you and I should expect Him to do the same thing for us. After all, this is God's M.O.! The Bible confirms it from front to back. In verse after verse, it says things like:

- Excuses might be found for a thief...But if he is caught, he will be fined seven times as much as he stole (Proverbs 6:30-31).
- Give fair judgment to the poor and the orphan; uphold the rights of the oppressed and the destitute. Rescue the poor and helpless; deliver them from the grasp of evil people (Psalm 82:3-4).
- I will give you back what you lost (Joel 2:25).
- I will take vengeance; I will repay those who deserve it (Romans 12:19).

God's love of justice will cause Him to provide recompense, restitution, or repayment for any damages the devil has inflicted on us. But we must open the door for it. If we want to receive the restoration God has promised, we have to do our part.

What, exactly, is our part?

Read what Jesus said in Luke 18 and you'll see. There, while encouraging His disciples to keep praying and not give up, He said this:

"There was in a certain city a judge who did not fear God nor regard man. Now there was a widow in that city; and she came to him, saying, 'Get justice for me from my adversary.' And he would not for a while; but afterward he said within himself, 'Though I do not fear God nor regard man, yet because this widow troubles me I will avenge her, lest by her continual coming she weary me.'" Then the Lord said, "Hear what the unjust judge said. And shall God not avenge His own elect who cry out day and night to Him, though He bears long with them? I tell you that He will avenge them speedily" (verses 2-8, NKJV).

To understand the point Jesus was making, the first thing you need settle is this: *God is not the unjust judge.* If you've been robbed, wronged, cheated, or mistreated in any way, He is not responsible for it. He has never, ever committed a single act of injustice.

According to the Bible, "righteousness and justice are the foundation of his throne."[171] Since the foundation is what holds everything up, if God ever became a party to injustice, His entire kingdom would collapse. His house would become divided and, as Jesus said, "[a] house divided against itself shall not stand."[172]

"Well, if God isn't the unjust judge in this situation," you might ask, "who is?"

The devil, of course! He's the mastermind behind everything that's been stolen from us, every answer to prayer that's been delayed, and every cry for justice that's been sabotaged. He's the culprit behind every evil plot and plan. And the feisty widow in this parable showed us how to deal with him.

She boldly, called for justice to be done!

She wasn't nice about it, either. She didn't make quiet, polite little requests. She was so determined to get what legally belonged to her that she got downright

---

[171] Psalm 97:2
[172] Matthew 12:25, KJV

fierce. She troubled the judge and wore him out. The Greek words used in the original Scriptures basically say that the widow applied pressure to him until she depleted his strength. She buffeted him as if she was a warrior. Metaphorically speaking, she hit him under the eye like a boxer until he was black and blue.

There wasn't anything timid about this widow. She was definitely sportin' an attitude!

> There wasn't anything timid about this widow. She was definitely sportin' an attitude! It's a good thing she was, too. Otherwise, that unjust judge would have ripped her off.

It's a good thing she was, too. Otherwise, that unjust judge would have ripped her off. Since he had no compassion and no fear of God, he would have gladly deprived her of the justice she was due if she hadn't verbally assaulted him day after day until he just...couldn't...take it...anymore.

If you think the widow's attitude doesn't sound very "Christian," think again. Jesus said that God's kingdom advances when "the violent take it by force."[173] He said His people receive the recompense they've been promised not just by whispering hopeful prayers, or by wishing God would intervene on their behalf, but by crying out "day and night" to be avenged of their adversary.

---

[173] Matthew 11:12, NKJV

According to the dictionary, when someone asks to be avenged, they are requesting immediate compensation to them for damages that have been caused. They're demanding that the perpetrator of the injustice that's been committed against them be forced to repay them for the losses they suffered.

That's what the widow in the parable did and we should do it too—with the same kind of persistence and boldness of faith!

Why are boldness and persistence so important?

Because that's what it takes to break through the devil's resistance. He's not going to give back what he's stolen from us just because it's right. He's a liar, a thief, and a bully. Like the unjust judge, he'll try to stonewall our demands for justice. So if we don't demand it, we won't get it. If we're timid in our prayers, he'll see to it that we get shoved to the back of the line.

On the other hand, just as a persistent drip, drip, drip of water will erode the hardest stone, our persistent declarations of faith in God's Word will wear down the devil until he has no strength to stand against us anymore.

USE YOUR VOICE
TO APPLY THE PRESSURE

Granted, this kind of audacious, insistent prayer isn't for the fainthearted. It requires spiritual fortitude. But that's okay, because God has provided it for us. He's said to us the same thing He said to Joshua when He told him to take the Promised Land:

"No one will be able to stand their ground against you as long as you live. For I will be with you...I will not fail you or abandon you. Be strong and courageous!" (Joshua 1:5-6).

Those words weren't just instructions to Joshua. They were carriers of God's power. Just as God created light in the Book of Genesis by saying, "Let there be light!" God released courage and strength to Joshua by saying, "Be strong and courageous!"

If you've read his story in the Bible, you know how Joshua responded. He believed God's Word, acted on it, and defeated every enemy that dared to come against him. He led the Israelites (who'd never had any military training) into battle after battle, conquered 31 kings and their kingdoms, and kept on conquering until God's people had possessed their God-given land.

We, as born again believers, can follow in Joshua's footsteps. We can receive the strength and courage God has given us and march forward in faith. Taking our stand on the Word and against the devil, we can take possession of the abundantly blessed life the Bible says is ours in Jesus' Name.

That's what I encourage you to do when you finish this book: Start using your voice to apply pressure day and night to the kingdom of darkness. Take your stand in the courtroom of heaven and say what God says about the justice that belongs to you. Declare His Word by faith, confident that God will do what He said and recompense you for whatever the devil has stolen from you through injustice, mistreatment, or betrayal.

If you'll do that, you can be sure you'll see results. God leaves no doubt about it. He said, "So shall My word be that goes forth from My mouth...it shall not return to Me void, But it shall accomplish what I please, And it shall prosper in the thing for which I sent it."[174]

Maybe the devil's attacks have cost you relationships. Maybe he's cheated you out of promotions at work. Maybe he's robbed you of respect and dignity, financial increase, or any number of other things. Don't be content to shrug off such losses. Don't just be glad you survived them. Go after the compensation God has promised you.

> Maybe the devil's attacks have cost you relationships. Maybe he's cheated you out of promotions at work. Don't be content to shrug off such losses.

Even if Satan, playing the role of the unjust judge, opposes you for a while, stick with it because he doesn't have the final say. There's a Greater Judge who has far more power than he. As Psalm 82 says:

> God presides over heaven's court; he pronounces judgment on the judges: "How long will you judges hand down unjust decisions?

---

[174] Isaiah 55:11, NKJV

How long will you shower special favors on the wicked? Give fair judgment to the poor and the orphan; uphold the rights of the oppressed and the destitute. Rescue the poor and helpless; deliver them from the grasp of evil people (verses 1-4).

God Almighty, your Heavenly Father, is the ultimate Judge, and it's His will for you to get justice. It's His will for the wrongs in your life to be made right again and for every evil thing the devil has used against you to be turned for your good.

But remember, we live in a voice activated system. God set it up that way. He said, "Whoever says to this mountain, 'Be removed and be cast into the sea,' and does not doubt in his heart, but believes that those things he says will be done, he will have whatever he says."[175]

What's more, He has given you authority and He expects you to use it. He said, "whatever you bind on earth will be bound in heaven, and whatever you loose on earth will be loosed in heaven."[176] So start speaking words of faith! Be like the widow and say them with such boldness and persistence they wear the devil out.

If you don't know how to get started, use the following prayer as your launching pad. I've used it in my own life many times.

---

[175] Mark 11:23, NKJV
[176] Matthew 16:19, NKJV

AVENGE US OF OUR ADVERSARY SPEEDILY

Heavenly Father, You are the just God of all the earth, sitting on Your throne, the High Court of Heaven. You execute justice for all who are oppressed. You are the God of angelic armies that fight against your enemies and avenge us of our adversaries. Because of Your great love toward us and Your love for justice, You have not forsaken us but You have come to our aid to uphold the justice upon Your throne in heaven.

The enemy has oppressed Your children. He has been resisting us, but now, Lord, we call upon You. Hear our cry, oh Lord, and be gracious and hearken to us. Restore justice in all of our situations. For You love justice and You hate robbery.

Bring Your righteous judgment upon our adversary and against all that he is doing. Punish and penalize him for what he has put us through—every suffering, every humiliation, every shame, every embarrassment, every fear, every hurt, every loss, every entrapment, every sickness, and every attack. The devil is the perpetrator. He is behind all the injustice we have experienced, so I pray in the Name of Jesus, deal with him and deliver us out of every affliction. Restore to us everything he has stolen from us and our ancestors.

Everything that has been delayed or withheld, come forth NOW! I command the release of open doors, opportunities, discoveries, inventions, business, organizations, creative ideas, relationships, favor, contracts, awards, promotions, and inheritance.

I bind the demonic spirits that have been working against me and I command the release of all the increase that has been fraudulently withheld, misdirected, sabotaged, blocked, stolen, and destroyed.

Lord, execute Your vengeance against the enemy SPEEDILY. Bring to us a full recompense that is due to us as redeemed heirs of God and joint heirs with Jesus Christ that we may advance Your kingdom in the earth. Crush the oppressor and all wickedness and establish Your justice among the Body of Christ.

We ask it by faith in the Name of Jesus!
Amen.

"...a masterpiece, written by the Master."
—**Kenneth Copeland**

"Whether you are weighed down by the past or exhausted...this book...will point you to freedom, peace, and abundant life."
—**John Bevere**

RECLAIM YOUR FREEDOM!

"FABULOUS! I've never read a book that dealt with so many issues in my personal life.... This book has taught me how to have a relationship with God as my Father for the first time in my Christian walk."
—**Bonnie Morentin**

"Wow, I am hanging on to every word. Thank you for writing this book."
—**Suzan Riebsomer**

"This book has helped me identify things in my own life that need healing. I appreciate your willingness to be REAL and honest about your struggles and feelings of inadequacy. That is what truly makes this book PRICELESS...."
—**Pastor Mike Vidaurri**

Surely this can't be so,

I thought as I read Vikki's openly exposing account of her life. As a teenager Vikki's spirit was rescued and set free by a new birth. Yet her pathetic past affected her soul.... [I]n this extremely well written, reads-like-a-novel book, she reveals how her deliverance came and how others can know complete victory and freedom."

—Billye Brim

Order today!

Call **1-800-742-4050** or
visit **DennisBurkeMinistries.org**

Also download in Kindle or ePub formats.

LIVE THE SATISFIED LIFE

every person can enjoy life the way God designed it—joy-filled and satisfying. Yet, there is a secret struggle affecting millions that shackles people to disappointment, discontent, and frustration. Even many "successful" people live quiet lives of desperation. They ask, "why am I overwhelmed and still so dissatisfied?"

In this life-changing book, Dr. Dennis Burke helps you identify controlling factors in your life that have held you back. Discover encouragement and insight from God's Word and the secrets of how to redefine your life.

There is a joy-filled life available to you. You really can live *The Satisfied Life*.

"THIS IS A POWERFUL TOOL. STUDY IT. MEDITATE IT."
—KENNETH COPELAND

Order
The Satisfied Life
1-800-742-4050

DennisBurkeMinistries.org

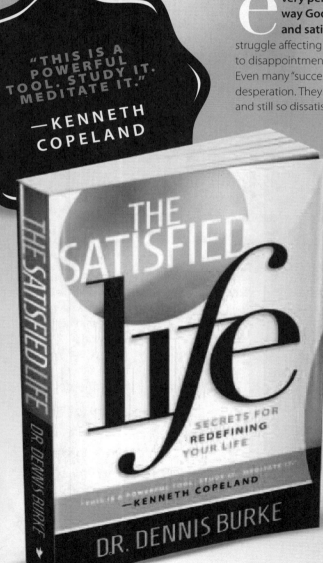

$14.99